C-3458

CAREER EXAMINATION SERIES

MAR 0 5 2021

THIS IS YOUR **PASSBOOK®** FOR ...

LABORER/ LABOR SUPERVISOR

NLC®

NATIONAL LEARNING CORPORATION®
passbooks.com

COPYRIGHT NOTICE

This book is SOLELY intended for, is sold ONLY to, and its use is RESTRICTED to individual, bona fide applicants or candidates who qualify by virtue of having seriously filed applications for appropriate license, certificate, professional and/or promotional advancement, higher school matriculation, scholarship, or other legitimate requirements of educational and/or governmental authorities.

This book is NOT intended for use, class instruction, tutoring, training, duplication, copying, reprinting, excerption, or adaptation, etc., by:

1) Other publishers
2) Proprietors and/or Instructors of «Coaching» and/or Preparatory Courses
3) Personnel and/or Training Divisions of commercial, industrial, and governmental organizations
4) Schools, colleges, or universities and/or their departments and staffs, including teachers and other personnel
5) Testing Agencies or Bureaus
6) Study groups which seek by the purchase of a single volume to copy and/or duplicate and/or adapt this material for use by the group as a whole without having purchased individual volumes for each of the members of the group
7) Et al.

Such persons would be in violation of appropriate Federal and State statutes.

PROVISION OF LICENSING AGREEMENTS. — Recognized educational, commercial, industrial, and governmental institutions and organizations, and others legitimately engaged in educational pursuits, including training, testing, and measurement activities, may address request for a licensing agreement to the copyright owners, who will determine whether, and under what conditions, including fees and charges, the materials in this book may be used them. In other words, a licensing facility exists for the legitimate use of the material in this book on other than an individual basis. However, it is asseverated and affirmed here that the material in this book CANNOT be used without the receipt of the express permission of such a licensing agreement from the Publishers. Inquiries re licensing should be addressed to the company, attention rights and permissions department.

All rights reserved, including the right of reproduction in whole or in part, in any form or by any means, electronic or mechanical, including photocopying, recording, or by any information storage and retrieval system, without permission in writing from the Publisher.

Copyright © 2020 by

National Learning Corporation

212 Michael Drive, Syosset, NY 11791
(516) 921-8888 • www.passbooks.com
E-mail: info@passbooks.com

PUBLISHED IN THE UNITED STATES OF AMERICA

PASSBOOK® SERIES

THE *PASSBOOK® SERIES* has been created to prepare applicants and candidates for the ultimate academic battlefield – the examination room.

At some time in our lives, each and every one of us may be required to take an examination – for validation, matriculation, admission, qualification, registration, certification, or licensure.

Based on the assumption that every applicant or candidate has met the basic formal educational standards, has taken the required number of courses, and read the necessary texts, the *PASSBOOK® SERIES* furnishes the one special preparation which may assure passing with confidence, instead of failing with insecurity. Examination questions – together with answers – are furnished as the basic vehicle for study so that the mysteries of the examination and its compounding difficulties may be eliminated or diminished by a sure method.

This book is meant to help you pass your examination provided that you qualify and are serious in your objective.

The entire field is reviewed through the huge store of content information which is succinctly presented through a provocative and challenging approach – the question-and-answer method.

A climate of success is established by furnishing the correct answers at the end of each test.

You soon learn to recognize types of questions, forms of questions, and patterns of questioning. You may even begin to anticipate expected outcomes.

You perceive that many questions are repeated or adapted so that you can gain acute insights, which may enable you to score many sure points.

You learn how to confront new questions, or types of questions, and to attack them confidently and work out the correct answers.

You note objectives and emphases, and recognize pitfalls and dangers, so that you may make positive educational adjustments.

Moreover, you are kept fully informed in relation to new concepts, methods, practices, and directions in the field.

You discover that you arre actually taking the examination all the time: you are preparing for the examination by "taking" an examination, not by reading extraneous and/or supererogatory textbooks.

In short, this PASSBOOK®, used directedly, should be an important factor in helping you to pass your test.

LABORER SUPERVISOR

DUTIES

A Labor Supervisor assigns, reviews and evaluates the work of a labor crew that may consist of helpers, laborers, semiskilled workers and equipment operators, and other employees engaged in various construction, maintenance, and repair projects, and other related duties; applies sound supervisory principles and techniques in building and maintaining an effective work force; and fulfills equal employment opportunity responsibilities. Responsible for ensuring that public works and related activities are done in an efficient manner, on schedule, and according to approved procedures. The incumbent performs related work as required.

SUBJECTS OF EXAMINATION:

The written test will be designed to evaluate knowledge, skills, and/or abilities in such areas as:

1. **Maintenance and Reconstruction of Streets, Sidewalks and Curbs** - These questions test for knowledge of the proper methods, materials and equipment used in the installation, repair and upkeep of street surfaces, utility access holes, gutters, catch basins, curbing and sidewalks, including ice and snow removal and control.

2. **Maintenance and Construction of Sanitary and Storm Sewer Systems** - These questions test for knowledge of the proper methods, materials and equipment used in the installation, maintenance, repair and cleaning of sanitary and storm sewers, catch basins and related appurtenances; and proper trenching and backfilling procedures.

3. **Safety Practices** - These questions test for knowledge of and the ability to apply safety principles related to construction and maintenance work zones, including traffic control, the safe use of equipment, and the overall safety of workers, the traveling public, and the work environment.

4. **Supervision** - These questions test for knowledge of the principles and practices employed in planning, organizing, and controlling the activities of a work unit toward predetermined objectives. The concepts covered, usually in a situational question format, include such topics as assigning and reviewing work; evaluating performance; maintaining work standards; motivating and developing subordinates; implementing procedural change; increasing efficiency; and dealing with problems of absenteeism, morale, and discipline.

5. **Mechanical Devices and Tools used in Maintenance Work** - These questions test for knowledge of general mechanical principles and for the ability to identify various types of hand tools and construction equipment and their proper use and maintenance.

HOW TO TAKE A TEST

I. YOU MUST PASS AN EXAMINATION

A. WHAT EVERY CANDIDATE SHOULD KNOW

Examination applicants often ask us for help in preparing for the written test. What can I study in advance? What kinds of questions will be asked? How will the test be given? How will the papers be graded?

As an applicant for a civil service examination, you may be wondering about some of these things. Our purpose here is to suggest effective methods of advance study and to describe civil service examinations.

Your chances for success on this examination can be increased if you know how to prepare. Those "pre-examination jitters" can be reduced if you know what to expect. You can even experience an adventure in good citizenship if you know why civil service exams are given.

B. WHY ARE CIVIL SERVICE EXAMINATIONS GIVEN?

Civil service examinations are important to you in two ways. As a citizen, you want public jobs filled by employees who know how to do their work. As a job seeker, you want a fair chance to compete for that job on an equal footing with other candidates. The best-known means of accomplishing this two-fold goal is the competitive examination.

Exams are widely publicized throughout the nation. They may be administered for jobs in federal, state, city, municipal, town or village governments or agencies.

Any citizen may apply, with some limitations, such as the age or residence of applicants. Your experience and education may be reviewed to see whether you meet the requirements for the particular examination. When these requirements exist, they are reasonable and applied consistently to all applicants. Thus, a competitive examination may cause you some uneasiness now, but it is your privilege and safeguard.

C. HOW ARE CIVIL SERVICE EXAMS DEVELOPED?

Examinations are carefully written by trained technicians who are specialists in the field known as "psychological measurement," in consultation with recognized authorities in the field of work that the test will cover. These experts recommend the subject matter areas or skills to be tested; only those knowledges or skills important to your success on the job are included. The most reliable books and source materials available are used as references. Together, the experts and technicians judge the difficulty level of the questions.

Test technicians know how to phrase questions so that the problem is clearly stated. Their ethics do not permit "trick" or "catch" questions. Questions may have been tried out on sample groups, or subjected to statistical analysis, to determine their usefulness.

Written tests are often used in combination with performance tests, ratings of training and experience, and oral interviews. All of these measures combine to form the best-known means of finding the right person for the right job.

II. HOW TO PASS THE WRITTEN TEST

A. NATURE OF THE EXAMINATION

To prepare intelligently for civil service examinations, you should know how they differ from school examinations you have taken. In school you were assigned certain definite pages to read or subjects to cover. The examination questions were quite detailed and usually emphasized memory. Civil service exams, on the other hand, try to discover your present ability to perform the duties of a position, plus your potentiality to learn these duties. In other words, a civil service exam attempts to predict how successful you will be. Questions cover such a broad area that they cannot be as minute and detailed as school exam questions.

In the public service similar kinds of work, or positions, are grouped together in one "class." This process is known as *position-classification*. All the positions in a class are paid according to the salary range for that class. One class title covers all of these positions, and they are all tested by the same examination.

B. FOUR BASIC STEPS

1) Study the announcement

How, then, can you know what subjects to study? Our best answer is: "Learn as much as possible about the class of positions for which you've applied." The exam will test the knowledge, skills and abilities needed to do the work.

Your most valuable source of information about the position you want is the official exam announcement. This announcement lists the training and experience qualifications. Check these standards and apply only if you come reasonably close to meeting them.

The brief description of the position in the examination announcement offers some clues to the subjects which will be tested. Think about the job itself. Review the duties in your mind. Can you perform them, or are there some in which you are rusty? Fill in the blank spots in your preparation.

Many jurisdictions preview the written test in the exam announcement by including a section called "Knowledge and Abilities Required," "Scope of the Examination," or some similar heading. Here you will find out specifically what fields will be tested.

2) Review your own background

Once you learn in general what the position is all about, and what you need to know to do the work, ask yourself which subjects you already know fairly well and which need improvement. You may wonder whether to concentrate on improving your strong areas or on building some background in your fields of weakness. When the announcement has specified "some knowledge" or "considerable knowledge," or has used adjectives like "beginning principles of…" or "advanced … methods," you can get a clue as to the number and difficulty of questions to be asked in any given field. More questions, and hence broader coverage, would be included for those subjects which are more important in the work. Now weigh your strengths and weaknesses against the job requirements and prepare accordingly.

3) Determine the level of the position

Another way to tell how intensively you should prepare is to understand the level of the job for which you are applying. Is it the entering level? In other words, is this the position in which beginners in a field of work are hired? Or is it an intermediate or advanced level? Sometimes this is indicated by such words as "Junior" or "Senior" in the class title. Other jurisdictions use Roman numerals to designate the level – Clerk I, Clerk II, for example. The word "Supervisor" sometimes appears in the title. If the level is not indicated by the title, check the description of duties. Will you be working under very close supervision, or will you have responsibility for independent decisions in this work?

4) Choose appropriate study materials

Now that you know the subjects to be examined and the relative amount of each subject to be covered, you can choose suitable study materials. For beginning level jobs, or even advanced ones, if you have a pronounced weakness in some aspect of your training, read a modern, standard textbook in that field. Be sure it is up to date and has general coverage. Such books are normally available at your library, and the librarian will be glad to help you locate one. For entry-level positions, questions of appropriate difficulty are chosen – neither highly advanced questions, nor those too simple. Such questions require careful thought but not advanced training.

If the position for which you are applying is technical or advanced, you will read more advanced, specialized material. If you are already familiar with the basic principles of your field, elementary textbooks would waste your time. Concentrate on advanced textbooks and technical periodicals. Think through the concepts and review difficult problems in your field.

These are all general sources. You can get more ideas on your own initiative, following these leads. For example, training manuals and publications of the government agency which employs workers in your field can be useful, particularly for technical and professional positions. A letter or visit to the government department involved may result in more specific study suggestions, and certainly will provide you with a more definite idea of the exact nature of the position you are seeking.

III. KINDS OF TESTS

Tests are used for purposes other than measuring knowledge and ability to perform specified duties. For some positions, it is equally important to test ability to make adjustments to new situations or to profit from training. In others, basic mental abilities not dependent on information are essential. Questions which test these things may not appear as pertinent to the duties of the position as those which test for knowledge and information. Yet they are often highly important parts of a fair examination. For very general questions, it is almost impossible to help you direct your study efforts. What we can do is to point out some of the more common of these general abilities needed in public service positions and describe some typical questions.

1) General information

Broad, general information has been found useful for predicting job success in some kinds of work. This is tested in a variety of ways, from vocabulary lists to questions about current events. Basic background in some field of work, such as sociology or economics, may be sampled in a group of questions. Often these are principles which have become familiar to most persons through exposure rather than through formal training. It is difficult to advise you how to study for these questions; being alert to the world around you is our best suggestion.

2) Verbal ability

An example of an ability needed in many positions is verbal or language ability. Verbal ability is, in brief, the ability to use and understand words. Vocabulary and grammar tests are typical measures of this ability. Reading comprehension or paragraph interpretation questions are common in many kinds of civil service tests. You are given a paragraph of written material and asked to find its central meaning.

3) Numerical ability

Number skills can be tested by the familiar arithmetic problem, by checking paired lists of numbers to see which are alike and which are different, or by interpreting charts and graphs. In the latter test, a graph may be printed in the test booklet which you are asked to use as the basis for answering questions.

4) Observation

A popular test for law-enforcement positions is the observation test. A picture is shown to you for several minutes, then taken away. Questions about the picture test your ability to observe both details and larger elements.

5) Following directions

In many positions in the public service, the employee must be able to carry out written instructions dependably and accurately. You may be given a chart with several columns, each column listing a variety of information. The questions require you to carry out directions involving the information given in the chart.

6) Skills and aptitudes

Performance tests effectively measure some manual skills and aptitudes. When the skill is one in which you are trained, such as typing or shorthand, you can practice. These tests are often very much like those given in business school or high school courses. For many of the other skills and aptitudes, however, no short-time preparation can be made. Skills and abilities natural to you or that you have developed throughout your lifetime are being tested.

Many of the general questions just described provide all the data needed to answer the questions and ask you to use your reasoning ability to find the answers. Your best preparation for these tests, as well as for tests of facts and ideas, is to be at your physical and mental best. You, no doubt, have your own methods of getting into an exam-taking mood and keeping "in shape." The next section lists some ideas on this subject.

IV. KINDS OF QUESTIONS

Only rarely is the "essay" question, which you answer in narrative form, used in civil service tests. Civil service tests are usually of the short-answer type. Full instructions for answering these questions will be given to you at the examination. But in case this is your first experience with short-answer questions and separate answer sheets, here is what you need to know:

1) Multiple-choice Questions

Most popular of the short-answer questions is the "multiple choice" or "best answer" question. It can be used, for example, to test for factual knowledge, ability to solve problems or judgment in meeting situations found at work.

A multiple-choice question is normally one of three types—
- It can begin with an incomplete statement followed by several possible endings. You are to find the one ending which *best* completes the statement, although some of the others may not be entirely wrong.
- It can also be a complete statement in the form of a question which is answered by choosing one of the statements listed.
- It can be in the form of a problem – again you select the best answer.

Here is an example of a multiple-choice question with a discussion which should give you some clues as to the method for choosing the right answer:

When an employee has a complaint about his assignment, the action which will *best* help him overcome his difficulty is to
- A. discuss his difficulty with his coworkers
- B. take the problem to the head of the organization
- C. take the problem to the person who gave him the assignment
- D. say nothing to anyone about his complaint

In answering this question, you should study each of the choices to find which is best. Consider choice "A" – Certainly an employee may discuss his complaint with fellow employees, but no change or improvement can result, and the complaint remains unresolved. Choice "B" is a poor choice since the head of the organization probably does not know what assignment you have been given, and taking your problem to him is known as "going over the head" of the supervisor. The supervisor, or person who made the assignment, is the person who can clarify it or correct any injustice. Choice "C" is, therefore, correct. To say nothing, as in choice "D," is unwise. Supervisors have and interest in knowing the problems employees are facing, and the employee is seeking a solution to his problem.

2) True/False Questions

The "true/false" or "right/wrong" form of question is sometimes used. Here a complete statement is given. Your job is to decide whether the statement is right or wrong.

SAMPLE: A roaming cell-phone call to a nearby city costs less than a non-roaming call to a distant city.

This statement is wrong, or false, since roaming calls are more expensive.

This is not a complete list of all possible question forms, although most of the others are variations of these common types. You will always get complete directions for answering questions. Be sure you understand *how* to mark your answers – ask questions until you do.

V. RECORDING YOUR ANSWERS

Computer terminals are used more and more today for many different kinds of exams.

For an examination with very few applicants, you may be told to record your answers in the test booklet itself. Separate answer sheets are much more common. If this separate answer sheet is to be scored by machine – and this is often the case – it is highly important that you mark your answers correctly in order to get credit.

An electronic scoring machine is often used in civil service offices because of the speed with which papers can be scored. Machine-scored answer sheets must be marked with a pencil, which will be given to you. This pencil has a high graphite content which responds to the electronic scoring machine. As a matter of fact, stray dots may register as answers, so do not let your pencil rest on the answer sheet while you are pondering the correct answer. Also, if your pencil lead breaks or is otherwise defective, ask for another.

Since the answer sheet will be dropped in a slot in the scoring machine, be careful not to bend the corners or get the paper crumpled.

The answer sheet normally has five vertical columns of numbers, with 30 numbers to a column. These numbers correspond to the question numbers in your test booklet. After each number, going across the page are four or five pairs of dotted lines. These short dotted lines have small letters or numbers above them. The first two pairs may also have a "T" or "F" above the letters. This indicates that the first two pairs only are to be used if the questions are of the true-false type. If the questions are multiple choice, disregard the "T" and "F" and pay attention only to the small letters or numbers.

Answer your questions in the manner of the sample that follows:

32. The largest city in the United States is
    A. Washington, D.C.
    B. New York City
    C. Chicago
    D. Detroit
    E. San Francisco

1) Choose the answer you think is best. (New York City is the largest, so "B" is correct.)
2) Find the row of dotted lines numbered the same as the question you are answering. (Find row number 32)
3) Find the pair of dotted lines corresponding to the answer. (Find the pair of lines under the mark "B.")
4) Make a solid black mark between the dotted lines.

VI. BEFORE THE TEST

Common sense will help you find procedures to follow to get ready for an examination. Too many of us, however, overlook these sensible measures. Indeed, nervousness and fatigue have been found to be the most serious reasons why applicants fail to do their best on civil service tests. Here is a list of reminders:

- Begin your preparation early – Don't wait until the last minute to go scurrying around for books and materials or to find out what the position is all about.
- Prepare continuously – An hour a night for a week is better than an all-night cram session. This has been definitely established. What is more, a night a week for a month will return better dividends than crowding your study into a shorter period of time.
- Locate the place of the exam – You have been sent a notice telling you when and where to report for the examination. If the location is in a different town or otherwise unfamiliar to you, it would be well to inquire the best route and learn something about the building.
- Relax the night before the test – Allow your mind to rest. Do not study at all that night. Plan some mild recreation or diversion; then go to bed early and get a good night's sleep.
- Get up early enough to make a leisurely trip to the place for the test – This way unforeseen events, traffic snarls, unfamiliar buildings, etc. will not upset you.
- Dress comfortably – A written test is not a fashion show. You will be known by number and not by name, so wear something comfortable.
- Leave excess paraphernalia at home – Shopping bags and odd bundles will get in your way. You need bring only the items mentioned in the official notice you received; usually everything you need is provided. Do not bring reference books to the exam. They will only confuse those last minutes and be taken away from you when in the test room.
- Arrive somewhat ahead of time – If because of transportation schedules you must get there very early, bring a newspaper or magazine to take your mind off yourself while waiting.
- Locate the examination room – When you have found the proper room, you will be directed to the seat or part of the room where you will sit. Sometimes you are given a sheet of instructions to read while you are waiting. Do not fill out any forms until you are told to do so; just read them and be prepared.
- Relax and prepare to listen to the instructions
- If you have any physical problem that may keep you from doing your best, be sure to tell the test administrator. If you are sick or in poor health, you really cannot do your best on the exam. You can come back and take the test some other time.

VII. AT THE TEST

The day of the test is here and you have the test booklet in your hand. The temptation to get going is very strong. Caution! There is more to success than knowing the right answers. You must know how to identify your papers and understand variations in the type of short-answer question used in this particular examination. Follow these suggestions for maximum results from your efforts:

1) Cooperate with the monitor

The test administrator has a duty to create a situation in which you can be as much at ease as possible. He will give instructions, tell you when to begin, check to see that you are marking your answer sheet correctly, and so on. He is not there to guard you, although he will see that your competitors do not take unfair advantage. He wants to help you do your best.

2) Listen to all instructions

Don't jump the gun! Wait until you understand all directions. In most civil service tests you get more time than you need to answer the questions. So don't be in a hurry. Read each word of instructions until you clearly understand the meaning. Study the examples, listen to all announcements and follow directions. Ask questions if you do not understand what to do.

3) Identify your papers

Civil service exams are usually identified by number only. You will be assigned a number; you must not put your name on your test papers. Be sure to copy your number correctly. Since more than one exam may be given, copy your exact examination title.

4) Plan your time

Unless you are told that a test is a "speed" or "rate of work" test, speed itself is usually not important. Time enough to answer all the questions will be provided, but this does not mean that you have all day. An overall time limit has been set. Divide the total time (in minutes) by the number of questions to determine the approximate time you have for each question.

5) Do not linger over difficult questions

If you come across a difficult question, mark it with a paper clip (useful to have along) and come back to it when you have been through the booklet. One caution if you do this – be sure to skip a number on your answer sheet as well. Check often to be sure that you have not lost your place and that you are marking in the row numbered the same as the question you are answering.

6) Read the questions

Be sure you know what the question asks! Many capable people are unsuccessful because they failed to *read* the questions correctly.

7) Answer all questions

Unless you have been instructed that a penalty will be deducted for incorrect answers, it is better to guess than to omit a question.

8) Speed tests

It is often better NOT to guess on speed tests. It has been found that on timed tests people are tempted to spend the last few seconds before time is called in marking answers at random – without even reading them – in the hope of picking up a few extra points. To discourage this practice, the instructions may warn you that your score will be "corrected" for guessing. That is, a penalty will be applied. The incorrect answers will be deducted from the correct ones, or some other penalty formula will be used.

9) Review your answers

If you finish before time is called, go back to the questions you guessed or omitted to give them further thought. Review other answers if you have time.

10) Return your test materials

If you are ready to leave before others have finished or time is called, take ALL your materials to the monitor and leave quietly. Never take any test material with you. The monitor can discover whose papers are not complete, and taking a test booklet may be grounds for disqualification.

VIII. EXAMINATION TECHNIQUES

1) Read the general instructions carefully. These are usually printed on the first page of the exam booklet. As a rule, these instructions refer to the timing of the examination; the fact that you should not start work until the signal and must stop work at a signal, etc. If there are any *special* instructions, such as a choice of questions to be answered, make sure that you note this instruction carefully.

2) When you are ready to start work on the examination, that is as soon as the signal has been given, read the instructions to each question booklet, underline any key words or phrases, such as *least, best, outline, describe* and the like. In this way you will tend to answer as requested rather than discover on reviewing your paper that you *listed without describing*, that you selected the *worst* choice rather than the *best* choice, etc.

3) If the examination is of the objective or multiple-choice type – that is, each question will also give a series of possible answers: A, B, C or D, and you are called upon to select the best answer and write the letter next to that answer on your answer paper – it is advisable to start answering each question in turn. There may be anywhere from 50 to 100 such questions in the three or four hours allotted and you can see how much time would be taken if you read through all the questions before beginning to answer any. Furthermore, if you come across a question or group of questions which you know would be difficult to answer, it would undoubtedly affect your handling of all the other questions.

4) If the examination is of the essay type and contains but a few questions, it is a moot point as to whether you should read all the questions before starting to answer any one. Of course, if you are given a choice – say five out of seven and the like – then it is essential to read all the questions so you can eliminate the two that are most difficult. If, however, you are asked to answer all the questions, there may be danger in trying to answer the easiest one first because you may find that you will spend too much time on it. The best technique is to answer the first question, then proceed to the second, etc.

5) Time your answers. Before the exam begins, write down the time it started, then add the time allowed for the examination and write down the time it must be completed, then divide the time available somewhat as follows:

- If 3-1/2 hours are allowed, that would be 210 minutes. If you have 80 objective-type questions, that would be an average of 2-1/2 minutes per question. Allow yourself no more than 2 minutes per question, or a total of 160 minutes, which will permit about 50 minutes to review.
- If for the time allotment of 210 minutes there are 7 essay questions to answer, that would average about 30 minutes a question. Give yourself only 25 minutes per question so that you have about 35 minutes to review.

6) The most important instruction is to *read each question* and make sure you know what is wanted. The second most important instruction is to *time yourself properly* so that you answer every question. The third most important instruction is to *answer every question.* Guess if you have to but include something for each question. Remember that you will receive no credit for a blank and will probably receive some credit if you write something in answer to an essay question. If you guess a letter – say "B" for a multiple-choice question – you may have guessed right. If you leave a blank as an answer to a multiple-choice question, the examiners may respect your feelings but it will not add a point to your score. Some exams may penalize you for wrong answers, so in such cases *only,* you may not want to guess unless you have some basis for your answer.

7) Suggestions
   a. Objective-type questions
      1. Examine the question booklet for proper sequence of pages and questions
      2. Read all instructions carefully
      3. Skip any question which seems too difficult; return to it after all other questions have been answered
      4. Apportion your time properly; do not spend too much time on any single question or group of questions
      5. Note and underline key words – *all, most, fewest, least, best, worst, same, opposite,* etc.
      6. Pay particular attention to negatives
      7. Note unusual option, e.g., unduly long, short, complex, different or similar in content to the body of the question
      8. Observe the use of "hedging" words – *probably, may, most likely,* etc.
      9. Make sure that your answer is put next to the same number as the question
      10. Do not second-guess unless you have good reason to believe the second answer is definitely more correct
      11. Cross out original answer if you decide another answer is more accurate; do not erase until you are ready to hand your paper in
      12. Answer all questions; guess unless instructed otherwise
      13. Leave time for review

   b. Essay questions
      1. Read each question carefully
      2. Determine exactly what is wanted. Underline key words or phrases.
      3. Decide on outline or paragraph answer

4. Include many different points and elements unless asked to develop any one or two points or elements
5. Show impartiality by giving pros and cons unless directed to select one side only
6. Make and write down any assumptions you find necessary to answer the questions
7. Watch your English, grammar, punctuation and choice of words
8. Time your answers; don't crowd material

8) Answering the essay question

Most essay questions can be answered by framing the specific response around several key words or ideas. Here are a few such key words or ideas:

M's: manpower, materials, methods, money, management
P's: purpose, program, policy, plan, procedure, practice, problems, pitfalls, personnel, public relations

a. Six basic steps in handling problems:
 1. Preliminary plan and background development
 2. Collect information, data and facts
 3. Analyze and interpret information, data and facts
 4. Analyze and develop solutions as well as make recommendations
 5. Prepare report and sell recommendations
 6. Install recommendations and follow up effectiveness

b. Pitfalls to avoid
 1. *Taking things for granted* – A statement of the situation does not necessarily imply that each of the elements is necessarily true; for example, a complaint may be invalid and biased so that all that can be taken for granted is that a complaint has been registered
 2. *Considering only one side of a situation* – Wherever possible, indicate several alternatives and then point out the reasons you selected the best one
 3. *Failing to indicate follow up* – Whenever your answer indicates action on your part, make certain that you will take proper follow-up action to see how successful your recommendations, procedures or actions turn out to be
 4. *Taking too long in answering any single question* – Remember to time your answers properly

IX. AFTER THE TEST

Scoring procedures differ in detail among civil service jurisdictions although the general principles are the same. Whether the papers are hand-scored or graded by machine we have described, they are nearly always graded by number. That is, the person who marks the paper knows only the number – never the name – of the applicant. Not until all the papers have been graded will they be matched with names. If other tests, such as training and experience or oral interview ratings have been given, scores will be combined. Different parts of the examination usually have different weights. For example, the written test might count 60 percent of the final grade, and a rating of training and experience 40 percent. In many jurisdictions, veterans will have a certain number of points added to their grades.

After the final grade has been determined, the names are placed in grade order and an eligible list is established. There are various methods for resolving ties between those who get the same final grade – probably the most common is to place first the name of the person whose application was received first. Job offers are made from the eligible list in the order the names appear on it. You will be notified of your grade and your rank as soon as all these computations have been made. This will be done as rapidly as possible.

People who are found to meet the requirements in the announcement are called "eligibles." Their names are put on a list of eligible candidates. An eligible's chances of getting a job depend on how high he stands on this list and how fast agencies are filling jobs from the list.

When a job is to be filled from a list of eligibles, the agency asks for the names of people on the list of eligibles for that job. When the civil service commission receives this request, it sends to the agency the names of the three people highest on this list. Or, if the job to be filled has specialized requirements, the office sends the agency the names of the top three persons who meet these requirements from the general list.

The appointing officer makes a choice from among the three people whose names were sent to him. If the selected person accepts the appointment, the names of the others are put back on the list to be considered for future openings.

That is the rule in hiring from all kinds of eligible lists, whether they are for typist, carpenter, chemist, or something else. For every vacancy, the appointing officer has his choice of any one of the top three eligibles on the list. This explains why the person whose name is on top of the list sometimes does not get an appointment when some of the persons lower on the list do. If the appointing officer chooses the second or third eligible, the No. 1 eligible does not get a job at once, but stays on the list until he is appointed or the list is terminated.

X. HOW TO PASS THE INTERVIEW TEST

The examination for which you applied requires an oral interview test. You have already taken the written test and you are now being called for the interview test – the final part of the formal examination.

You may think that it is not possible to prepare for an interview test and that there are no procedures to follow during an interview. Our purpose is to point out some things you can do in advance that will help you and some good rules to follow and pitfalls to avoid while you are being interviewed.

What is an interview supposed to test?

The written examination is designed to test the technical knowledge and competence of the candidate; the oral is designed to evaluate intangible qualities, not readily measured otherwise, and to establish a list showing the relative fitness of each candidate – as measured against his competitors – for the position sought. Scoring is not on the basis of "right" and "wrong," but on a sliding scale of values ranging from "not passable" to "outstanding." As a matter of fact, it is possible to achieve a relatively low score without a single "incorrect" answer because of evident weakness in the qualities being measured.

Occasionally, an examination may consist entirely of an oral test – either an individual or a group oral. In such cases, information is sought concerning the technical knowledges and abilities of the candidate, since there has been no written examination for this purpose. More commonly, however, an oral test is used to supplement a written examination.

Who conducts interviews?

The composition of oral boards varies among different jurisdictions. In nearly all, a representative of the personnel department serves as chairman. One of the members of the board may be a representative of the department in which the candidate would work. In some cases, "outside experts" are used, and, frequently, a businessman or some other representative of the general public is asked to serve. Labor and management or other special groups may be represented. The aim is to secure the services of experts in the appropriate field.

However the board is composed, it is a good idea (and not at all improper or unethical) to ascertain in advance of the interview who the members are and what groups they represent. When you are introduced to them, you will have some idea of their backgrounds and interests, and at least you will not stutter and stammer over their names.

What should be done before the interview?

While knowledge about the board members is useful and takes some of the surprise element out of the interview, there is other preparation which is more substantive. It *is* possible to prepare for an oral interview – in several ways:

1) Keep a copy of your application and review it carefully before the interview

This may be the only document before the oral board, and the starting point of the interview. Know what education and experience you have listed there, and the sequence and dates of all of it. Sometimes the board will ask you to review the highlights of your experience for them; you should not have to hem and haw doing it.

2) Study the class specification and the examination announcement

Usually, the oral board has one or both of these to guide them. The qualities, characteristics or knowledges required by the position sought are stated in these documents. They offer valuable clues as to the nature of the oral interview. For example, if the job involves supervisory responsibilities, the announcement will usually indicate that knowledge of modern supervisory methods and the qualifications of the candidate as a supervisor will be tested. If so, you can expect such questions, frequently in the form of a hypothetical situation which you are expected to solve. NEVER go into an oral without knowledge of the duties and responsibilities of the job you seek.

3) Think through each qualification required

Try to visualize the kind of questions you would ask if you were a board member. How well could you answer them? Try especially to appraise your own knowledge and background in each area, *measured against the job sought*, and identify any areas in which you are weak. Be critical and realistic – do not flatter yourself.

4) Do some general reading in areas in which you feel you may be weak

For example, if the job involves supervision and your past experience has NOT, some general reading in supervisory methods and practices, particularly in the field of human relations, might be useful. Do NOT study agency procedures or detailed manuals. The oral board will be testing your understanding and capacity, not your memory.

5) Get a good night's sleep and watch your general health and mental attitude

You will want a clear head at the interview. Take care of a cold or any other minor ailment, and of course, no hangovers.

What should be done on the day of the interview?

Now comes the day of the interview itself. Give yourself plenty of time to get there. Plan to arrive somewhat ahead of the scheduled time, particularly if your appointment is in the fore part of the day. If a previous candidate fails to appear, the board might be ready for you a bit early. By early afternoon an oral board is almost invariably behind schedule if there are many candidates, and you may have to wait. Take along a book or magazine to read, or your application to review, but leave any extraneous material in the waiting room when you go in for your interview. In any event, relax and compose yourself.

The matter of dress is important. The board is forming impressions about you – from your experience, your manners, your attitude, and your appearance. Give your personal appearance careful attention. Dress your best, but not your flashiest. Choose conservative, appropriate clothing, and be sure it is immaculate. This is a business interview, and your appearance should indicate that you regard it as such. Besides, being well groomed and properly dressed will help boost your confidence.

Sooner or later, someone will call your name and escort you into the interview room. *This is it.* From here on you are on your own. It is too late for any more preparation. But remember, you asked for this opportunity to prove your fitness, and you are here because your request was granted.

What happens when you go in?

The usual sequence of events will be as follows: The clerk (who is often the board stenographer) will introduce you to the chairman of the oral board, who will introduce you to the other members of the board. Acknowledge the introductions before you sit down. Do not be surprised if you find a microphone facing you or a stenotypist sitting by. Oral interviews are usually recorded in the event of an appeal or other review.

Usually the chairman of the board will open the interview by reviewing the highlights of your education and work experience from your application – primarily for the benefit of the other members of the board, as well as to get the material into the record. Do not interrupt or comment unless there is an error or significant misinterpretation; if that is the case, do not hesitate. But do not quibble about insignificant matters. Also, he will usually ask you some question about your education, experience or your present job – partly to get you to start talking and to establish the interviewing "rapport." He may start the actual questioning, or turn it over to one of the other members. Frequently, each member undertakes the questioning on a particular area, one in which he is perhaps most competent, so you can expect each member to participate in the examination. Because time is limited, you may also expect some rather abrupt switches in the direction the questioning takes, so do not be upset by it. Normally, a board member will not pursue a single line of questioning unless he discovers a particular strength or weakness.

After each member has participated, the chairman will usually ask whether any member has any further questions, then will ask you if you have anything you wish to add. Unless you are expecting this question, it may floor you. Worse, it may start you off on an extended, extemporaneous speech. The board is not usually seeking more information. The question is principally to offer you a last opportunity to present further qualifications or to indicate that you have nothing to add. So, if you feel that a significant qualification or characteristic has been overlooked, it is proper to point it out in a sentence or so. Do not compliment the board on the thoroughness of their examination – they have been sketchy, and you know it. If you wish, merely say, "No thank you, I have nothing further to add." This is a point where you can "talk yourself out" of a good impression or fail to present an important bit of information. Remember, *you close the interview yourself.*

The chairman will then say, "That is all, Mr. _____, thank you." Do not be startled; the interview is over, and quicker than you think. Thank him, gather your belongings and take your leave. Save your sigh of relief for the other side of the door.

How to put your best foot forward

Throughout this entire process, you may feel that the board individually and collectively is trying to pierce your defenses, seek out your hidden weaknesses and embarrass and confuse you. Actually, this is not true. They are obliged to make an appraisal of your qualifications for the job you are seeking, and they want to see you in your best light. Remember, they must interview all candidates and a non-cooperative candidate may become a failure in spite of their best efforts to bring out his qualifications. Here are 15 suggestions that will help you:

1) Be natural – Keep your attitude confident, not cocky

If you are not confident that you can do the job, do not expect the board to be. Do not apologize for your weaknesses, try to bring out your strong points. The board is interested in a positive, not negative, presentation. Cockiness will antagonize any board member and make him wonder if you are covering up a weakness by a false show of strength.

2) Get comfortable, but don't lounge or sprawl

Sit erectly but not stiffly. A careless posture may lead the board to conclude that you are careless in other things, or at least that you are not impressed by the importance of the occasion. Either conclusion is natural, even if incorrect. Do not fuss with your clothing, a pencil or an ashtray. Your hands may occasionally be useful to emphasize a point; do not let them become a point of distraction.

3) Do not wisecrack or make small talk

This is a serious situation, and your attitude should show that you consider it as such. Further, the time of the board is limited – they do not want to waste it, and neither should you.

4) Do not exaggerate your experience or abilities

In the first place, from information in the application or other interviews and sources, the board may know more about you than you think. Secondly, you probably will not get away with it. An experienced board is rather adept at spotting such a situation, so do not take the chance.

5) If you know a board member, do not make a point of it, yet do not hide it

Certainly you are not fooling him, and probably not the other members of the board. Do not try to take advantage of your acquaintanceship – it will probably do you little good.

6) Do not dominate the interview

Let the board do that. They will give you the clues – do not assume that you have to do all the talking. Realize that the board has a number of questions to ask you, and do not try to take up all the interview time by showing off your extensive knowledge of the answer to the first one.

7) Be attentive

You only have 20 minutes or so, and you should keep your attention at its sharpest throughout. When a member is addressing a problem or question to you, give him your undivided attention. Address your reply principally to him, but do not exclude the other board members.

8) Do not interrupt

A board member may be stating a problem for you to analyze. He will ask you a question when the time comes. Let him state the problem, and wait for the question.

9) Make sure you understand the question

Do not try to answer until you are sure what the question is. If it is not clear, restate it in your own words or ask the board member to clarify it for you. However, do not haggle about minor elements.

10) Reply promptly but not hastily

A common entry on oral board rating sheets is "candidate responded readily," or "candidate hesitated in replies." Respond as promptly and quickly as you can, but do not jump to a hasty, ill-considered answer.

11) Do not be peremptory in your answers

A brief answer is proper – but do not fire your answer back. That is a losing game from your point of view. The board member can probably ask questions much faster than you can answer them.

12) Do not try to create the answer you think the board member wants

He is interested in what kind of mind you have and how it works – not in playing games. Furthermore, he can usually spot this practice and will actually grade you down on it.

13) Do not switch sides in your reply merely to agree with a board member

Frequently, a member will take a contrary position merely to draw you out and to see if you are willing and able to defend your point of view. Do not start a debate, yet do not surrender a good position. If a position is worth taking, it is worth defending.

14) Do not be afraid to admit an error in judgment if you are shown to be wrong

The board knows that you are forced to reply without any opportunity for careful consideration. Your answer may be demonstrably wrong. If so, admit it and get on with the interview.

15) Do not dwell at length on your present job

The opening question may relate to your present assignment. Answer the question but do not go into an extended discussion. You are being examined for a *new* job, not your present one. As a matter of fact, try to phrase ALL your answers in terms of the job for which you are being examined.

Basis of Rating

Probably you will forget most of these "do's" and "don'ts" when you walk into the oral interview room. Even remembering them all will not ensure you a passing grade. Perhaps you did not have the qualifications in the first place. But remembering them will help you to put your best foot forward, without treading on the toes of the board members.

Rumor and popular opinion to the contrary notwithstanding, an oral board wants you to make the best appearance possible. They know you are under pressure – but they also want to see how you respond to it as a guide to what your reaction would be under the pressures of the job you seek. They will be influenced by the degree of poise you display, the personal traits you show and the manner in which you respond.

ABOUT THIS BOOK

This book contains tests divided into Examination Sections. Go through each test, answering every question in the margin. At the end of each test look at the answer key and check your answers. On the ones you got wrong, look at the right answer choice and learn. Do not fill in the answers first. Do not memorize the questions and answers, but understand the answer and principles involved. On your test, the questions will likely be different from the samples. Questions are changed and new ones added. If you understand these past questions you should have success with any changes that arise. Tests may consist of several types of questions. We have additional books on each subject should more study be advisable or necessary for you. Finally, the more you study, the better prepared you will be. This book is intended to be the last thing you study before you walk into the examination room. Prior study of relevant texts is also recommended. NLC publishes some of these in our Fundamental Series. Knowledge and good sense are important factors in passing your exam. Good luck also helps. So now study this Passbook, absorb the material contained within and take that knowledge into the examination. Then do your best to pass that exam.

EXAMINATION SECTION

EXAMINATION SECTION
TEST 1

DIRECTIONS: Each question or incomplete statement is followed by several suggested answers or completions. Select the one that BEST answers the question or completes the statement. *PRINT THE LETTER OF THE CORRECT ANSWER IN THE SPACE AT THE RIGHT.*

1. On the monthly report of the amount of work completed, the units used to measure the amount of work completed on guardrails and beam barriers installed on arterial highways is

    A. square feet
    B. square yards
    C. linear feet
    D. linear yards

2. On the daily work report for the sidewalk concrete gang is a formula, $M = [G - (D + U)]$, where G = total man-hours worked, D = total man-hours delays, U = total man-hours unmeasured work, and M = total man-hours measured work.
If G = 98, D = 42, U = 21, then M is equal to

    A. 35   B. 56   C. 77   D. 119

3. When a plumber *opens a street*, he is responsible for restoring the pavement. After completion of the permanent restoration, the plumber is responsible for maintaining the restored area for a total period of

    A. six months
    B. one year
    C. one year and 6 months
    D. two years

4. A permit for a street opening may be issued for a single permit activity for one block length up to a MAXIMUM length of _____ feet.

    A. 50   B. 100   C. 200   D. 300

5. A street obstruction bond taken out by a contractor working in the street is to insure the city if

    A. a pedestrian is injured by material stored on the sidewalk
    B. an automobile is damaged by material stored in the street
    C. curbs, sidewalks, and pavements are damaged
    D. obstructions, illegally placed in the street, must be removed

6. On the daily work report for the sidewalk concrete gang is an item *curb*.
The different types of curb listed on the report are: bluestone or granite, concrete-steel face, concrete-regular face, and

    A. drop
    B. paving block
    C. concrete block
    D. prefabricated

7. On the monthly report of work output under time (manhours) is a column headed MSO, which refers to manhours

    A. of mechanical services operator other than MVO
    B. of operation time lost while waiting
    C. of operation time lost due to the weather
    D. spent operating mechanical equipment by the MVO

8. In the city, concrete sidewalks are required to have a minimum thickness of concrete of _____ inches.

   A. 3   B. 4   C. 5   D. 6

9. Asphalt was laid for a length of 210 feet on the entire width of a street whose curb-to-curb distance is 30 feet. The number of square yards covered with asphalt is MOST NEARLY

   A. 210   B. 700   C. 2100   D. 6300

10. A layer of cinders is used as a base for a concrete sidewalk.
    The MAIN purpose of the cinders is to

    A. act as an air entraining agent for the concrete in the sidewalk
    B. replace poor soil under the sidewalk
    C. provide drainage under the sidewalk
    D. cushion the sidewalk when heavy loads are placed on the sidewalk

11. The unit used on the daily gang report to report the amount of measurement of debris removed is

    A. square foot   B. square yard
    C. cubic foot   D. cubic yard

12. 627 cubic feet contains MOST NEARLY _____ cubic yards.

    A. 21   B. 22   C. 23   D. 24

13. Of the following, the one that is INCORRECT curb construction is a curb made

    A. with a height of 5 inches
    B. with a steel angle for the face
    C. without a steel face
    D. monolithically with the sidewalk

14. Where feasible, concrete sidewalk panels should be made in squares of _____ feet by _____ feet.

    A. 3; 3   B. 5; 5   C. 6; 6   D. 7; 7

15. The steel facing for concrete curbs are splayed

    A. at an expansion joint
    B. where it butts against an adjacent steel plate
    C. at a drop curb
    D. at a radius bend

16. Expansion joints in steel curb facing shall be 1/4 inch wide and shall be filled with

    A. sand   B. premolded filler
    C. poured asphalt   D. dry pack

17. One inch is MOST NEARLY equal to _____ feet.

    A. 0.8   B. 0.08   C. 0.008   D. 0.0008

18. Of the following, the *final* finish on a sidewalk is MOST frequently made with a

    A. wood float
    B. screed
    C. steel trowel
    D. darby

19. An air entraining compound would be added to concrete MAINLY to

    A. make the concrete lighter
    B. make the concrete cure faster
    C. improve the resistance of the concrete to frost action
    D. increase the tensile strength of the concrete

20. *ASTM,* as used in specifications for concrete, is an abbreviation for the

    A. American Society for Testing Materials
    B. American Standard Training Manual
    C. American Standard Testing Materials
    D. Association of Scientists for Testing Materials

21. A 15-foot-wide sidewalk has a pitch of 1/4 inch per foot. The difference in elevation from the curb to 15 feet from the curb in the direction of the pitch is _____ inches.

    A. 3   B. 3 3/4   C. 4   D. 4 1/2

22. A liquid asphalt is designated *RC70*.
    The letters RC stand for

    A. Rough Course
    B. Rubber Cement
    C. Rapid Curing
    D. Reinforced Concrete

23. Unless otherwise specified, steel faced concrete curb shall consist of the steel curb facing in _____-foot lengths.

    A. 5   B. 10   C. 15   D. 20

24. The difference between sheet asphalt and asphaltic concrete is that sheet asphalt

    A. contains no sand while asphaltic concrete contains sand
    B. contains no coarse aggregate while asphaltic concrete contains coarse aggregate
    C. contains no mineral filler while asphaltic concrete contains mineral filler
    D. has no flux while asphaltic concrete has flux

25. An approved roller shall weigh not less than 225 pounds per inch width of main roll. If the main roll width is 60 inches, the MINIMUM roller weight shall be equal to or greater than _____ lbs.

    A. 12,000   B. 12,500   C. 13,000   D. 13,500

KEY (CORRECT ANSWERS)

1. C
2. A
3. D
4. D
5. C

6. A
7. A
8. B
9. B
10. C

11. D
12. C
13. D
14. B
15. C

16. B
17. B
18. A
19. C
20. A

21. B
22. C
23. D
24. B
25. D

TEST 2

DIRECTIONS: Each question or incomplete statement is followed by several suggested answers or completions. Select the one that BEST answers the question or completes the statement. *PRINT THE LETTER OF THE CORRECT ANSWER IN THE SPACE AT THE RIGHT.*

1. A specification states that the rate of application of asphalt cement shall be 1 1/2 gallons per square yard with a tolerance of 1/10 of a gallon.
   Of the following, the rate of application that would be acceptable is _____ gallons per square yard.

   A. 1.2   B. 1.3   C. 1.6   D. 1.7

   1._____

2. Of the following, the BEST reason for compacting backfill is to

   A. prevent settlement
   B. crush oversized rocks
   C. facilitate drainage
   D. make the soil uniform

   2._____

3. Asphalt block is hexagonal tile block.
   The number of vertical sides of each block in place is

   A. 4   B. 6   C. 8   D. 10

   3._____

4. Concrete driveways shall have a MINIMUM thickness of concrete of _____ inches.

   A. 5   B. 6   C. 7   D. 8

   4._____

5. When the tops of manholes must be raised because of repaving, the MOST practical of the following methods to use is to

   A. break out the manhole frame and replace it with a deeper frame
   B. remove the manhole frame, build up the top of the manhole with bricks, and reset the frame
   C. use a thicker manhole cover
   D. place a metal collar on top of the existing frame

   5._____

6. In a 1:2:4 concrete mix, the 2 indicates the quantity of

   A. water   B. sand   C. cement   D. aggregate

   6._____

7. A tree pit shall be located in the area immediately in back of the curb.
   The MAXIMUM size of the tree pit shall be

   A. 3' x 3'   B. 4' x 4'   C. 5' x 5'   D. 6' x 6'

   7._____

8. A temporary asphaltic pavement is placed over an excavation in the street by a private contractor.
   The MINIMUM required thickness of the finish course of the temporary asphaltic pavement is _____ inch(es).

   A. 1   B. 2   C. 3   D. 4

   8._____

9. When a vault is abandoned, it must be filled in with clean incombustible materials, well-tamped.
   Where such structures adjoin the curb of a street, the roof must be removed and the enclosing walls cut down below the curb to a depth of _____ feet.

   A. 2   B. 4   C. 6   D. 8

   9._____

10. Granite curbs are required to be set on a cradle. The MAIN purpose of the cradle is to

 A. prevent cracking of the curb
 B. prevent settling of the curb
 C. help keep the curb in line while it is being set
 D. separate the curb from the adjacent sidewalk

11. Paving was installed on a street from Station 3+15 to Station 4+90.
 The length of street that was paved is _____ feet.

 A. 75 B. 115 C. 175 D. 215

12. A district foreman uses an engineer's tape and measures a distance of 26.50 feet. This distance is equal to _____ feet _____ inch(es).

 A. 26; 5 B. 26; 6 C. 26; 1/2 D. 26; 0.6

13. Written on a can containing material delivered from a manufacturer is the notation *Approved by the B.S. & A.*
 The B.S. & A. is an abbreviation for the

 A. Bureau of Shipping and Allocation
 B. Board of Standards and Appeals
 C. Board of Supervision and Approval
 D. Bureau of Supervision and Assistance

14. An asphalt macadam pavement consists of a base course and a wearing course. The purpose of the base course is to

 A. provide drainage
 B. provide a level surface for the wearing course
 C. spread the load from the surface when it reaches the soil
 D. replace defective soil

15. Of the following, the MOST important recent advancement in power-driven equipment and tools is

 A. reduction in weight of the equipment
 B. improved surface finish
 C. higher operating speed
 D. lower noise levels

16. A wooden horse, used to warn traffic away, should be placed in front of which of the following defects in the street?
 A

 A. broken curb
 B. piece of roadway pavement that is very thin and the pavement whose base is starting to show through
 C. very badly broken manhole cover in the center of the street
 D. catch basin filled to the surface with debris

17. When a street is to be paved, the roller should

    A. start at the curb, go the length of the street and then move toward the center
    B. move from curb to curb transversely across the street
    C. start at the center, go the length of the street, and then move toward the curb
    D. roll at all the manhole covers first and then start rolling the length of the street

18. The use of long chutes to place concrete for a road base is usually prohibited.
    The BEST of the following reasons for prohibiting long chutes in this case is that

    A. the concrete will set by the time it is in place
    B. the water will evaporate from the mix
    C. segregation of the aggregate will occur
    D. the stone will be broken down into smaller particles

19. When sheet asphalt is spread by hand, the speed of the rolling should NOT exceed _____ square yards per hour.

    A. 100   B. 300   C. 500   D. 700

20. Of the following, the BEST way to insure long trouble-free operation of mechanical equipment is by periodic inspection and

    A. use   B. servicing
    C. painting   D. rotation of operators

21. Of the following maintenance work, the one type that is LEAST likely to be done by your agency on mechanical equipment is

    A. tune-up   B. repairing
    C. overhauling   D. rebuilding

22. Of the following, the MOST important equipment needed to lay sheet asphalt pavement is truck, roller, fire wagon, and

    A. grader   B. distributor
    C. planer   D. spreader

23. Of the following, the BEST reason why deep potholes should be repaired *immediately* is that

    A. they look bad
    B. they are a safety hazard
    C. they present a drainage problem
    D. people complaining about unfilled potholes cause unfavorable publicity

24. Of the following, the MOST serious safety hazard on highway and street maintenance work is

    A. injury from flying debris during pavement breaking
    B. motor traffic
    C. working close to trucks, bulldozers, and rollers
    D. cave-ins

25. Of the following, the BEST way a laborer can avoid accidents is to 25.____

    A. work slowly
    B. be alert
    C. wear safety shoes
    D. wear glasses

26. Of the following, the BEST first aid treatment for a second degree burn is to cover the burn with a _____ sterile dressing. 26.____

    A. thin, wet
    B. thin, dry
    C. thick, wet
    D. thick, dry

27. One of the laborers on the job feels unusually tired, has a headache and nausea, is perspiring heavily, and the skin is pale and clammy. 27.____
    He is probably suffering from

    A. epilepsy
    B. food poisoning
    C. heat exhaustion
    D. sunstroke

28. If a laborer feels faint, the BEST advice to give him is to advise him to 28.____

    A. lie flat with his head low
    B. walk around till he revives
    C. run around till he revives
    D. drink a glass of cold water

29. Of the following types of fire extinguisher, the one to use on an electrical fire is 29.____

    A. soda acid
    B. carbon dioxide
    C. water pump tank
    D. pyrene

30. The GREATEST number of injuries from equipment used in construction work result from 30.____

    A. carelessness of the operator
    B. poor maintenance of the equipment
    C. overloading of the equipment
    D. poor inspection of the equipment

KEY (CORRECT ANSWERS)

1.	C	16.	C
2.	A	17.	A
3.	B	18.	C
4.	C	19.	B
5.	D	20.	B
6.	B	21.	D
7.	C	22.	D
8.	C	23.	B
9.	A	24.	B
10.	B	25.	B
11.	C	26.	D
12.	B	27.	C
13.	B	28.	A
14.	C	29.	B
15.	D	30.	A

EXAMINATION SECTION
TEST 1

DIRECTIONS: Each question or incomplete statement is followed by several suggested answers or completions. Select the one that BEST answers the question or completes the statement. *PRINT THE LETTER OF THE CORRECT ANSWER IN THE SPACE AT THE RIGHT.*

1. To prevent asphalt from sticking to the inner surfaces of a dump truck, the surfaces should be sprayed with   1.____

   A. gasoline
   B. water
   C. kerosene
   D. heavy fuel oil

2. A pneumatic roller   2.____

   A. is steam powered
   B. has rubber tires
   C. has steel rolls
   D. is diesel powered

3. A trench is 4'0" wide by 8'6" deep by 48'0" long. The volume of earth removed to form this trench, in cubic yards, is MOST NEARLY   3.____

   A. 62   B. 60   C. 58   D. 56

4. The presence of lumps in a sheet asphalt mixture is MOST likely an indication that the mixture   4.____

   A. is too cold
   B. is too hot
   C. does not contain enough asphaltic cement
   D. contains too much sand

5. The bedding material for granite block pavement is usually   5.____

   A. asphalt
   B. concrete
   C. sand
   D. mineral dust

6. Cold patch asphalt is usually shipped by the manufacturer in   6.____

   A. steel drums
   B. wooden kegs
   C. cloth sacks
   D. aluminum sacks

7. The proper drainage of a street is LEAST dependent upon the _____ the street.   7.____

   A. crown of
   B. gutters of
   C. manholes in
   D. inlets of

8. The dead end of a vitrified pipe sewer should   8.____

   A. be closed with a bulkhead of brick masonry
   B. be closed with a wooden bulkhead
   C. have a cast iron gate valve
   D. be left open

9. The ONLY portions of vitrified pipe which should be left partly unglazed or scored with parallel lines are the _____ spigot.   9.____

A. *outside* of the hub and the inside of the
B. *inside* of the hub and the outside of the
C. *outside* of both hub and
D. *inside* of both hub and

10. A manhole cover which had few or no openings would MOST likely be used on a manhole built

 A. for a sanitary sewer
 B. for a combined sewer
 C. for a storm sewer
 D. under a sidewalk

11. Bituminous material is normally used to make joints in sewer pipe when the sewer is a _____ sewer _____ the normal water table.

 A. sanitary; above
 B. sanitary; alongside
 C. storm; above
 D. storm; below

12. Assume that Class A concrete is a 1:2:4 mix with 6 gallons of water per sack of cement, and Class B concrete is a 1:2 1/2:5 mix with 6 gallons of water per sack of cement.
With reference to the foregoing, the statement MOST NEARLY correct is that the

 A. Class A concrete is much stronger
 B. Class B concrete is much stronger
 C. number of cubic feet of concrete per sack of cement is greater for the Class A concrete
 D. number of cubic feet of concrete per sack of cement is greater for the Class B concrete

13. When fresh concrete is to be placed on concrete that has already set, the one of the following procedures which would be MOST accurate is that the existing surface of concrete should be

 A. cleaned
 B. cleaned and wet down
 C. cleaned, wet down, and roughened
 D. cleaned, wet down, roughened, and coated with a grout of neat cement

14. Assume that a specification reads: Bats may be used in inside ring of arch and inverts for closers only.
The bats referred to are usually made of

 A. concrete   B. wood   C. brick   D. metal

15. Other things being equal, close sheeting is MOST likely to be required in trenches which are

 A. shallow   B. deep   C. wide   D. narrow

16. Assume that a foreman on a trenching job insists that the road surface adjacent to the trench be swept periodically.
It is MOST likely that his reason for doing so is PRIMARILY based on consideration of

 A. appearance
 B. safety
 C. fussiness
 D. keeping someone busy

17. The head of a bar that was used to break concrete has been redressed and tempered. This is usually

   A. *good* practice, because a mushroomed head is dangerous
   B. *bad* practice, because it should not have been tempered
   C. *good* practice, because it restores the bar to its original condition
   D. *bad* practice, because it adds to the cost of the job

18. When lifting a heavy object, a man should NOT

   A. keep his back straight and vertical
   B. place his feet wide apart
   C. bend at the knees to grasp the object
   D. get a firm hold on the object

19. Ignoring the overlap, the length, in inches, of the gasket for a gasket and mortar joint on a 12-inch (internal diameter) pipe with a wall thickness of 1 inch is MOST NEARLY

   A. 38   B. 41   C. 44   D. 47

20. The mortar that is used for a gasket and mortar joint on a vitrified pipe sewer is

   A. neat cement grout
   B. 1 part cement, 1 to 1 1/2 parts sand, mixed with water
   C. 1 part cement, 3 parts sand, mixed with water
   D. 1 part cement, 1 part sand, 1 part gravel, mixed with water

21. The MOST important function performed by the gasket in a gasket and mortar joint is to

   A. keep the mortar out of the pipe
   B. reduce the quantity of mortar used
   C. keep the spigot centered in the hub
   D. provide a cushion when the mortar is being rammed

22. The length of a single section of sewer rod that is used for cleaning is usually limited by

   A. weight considerations
   B. the strength of the material used for the rod
   C. the size of manhole cover
   D. the diameter of manhole at sewer elevation

23. Aside from safety considerations, the MOST important function of close sheeting in trenching is to

   A. prevent undermining of adjacent pavement
   B. improve the appearance of the job
   C. make it easier to use excavating machinery
   D. keep out water

24. Assume that a pump is being used to pump out a deep cellar which has been flooded. Of the following distances, the one which will MOST likely prevent the operation of the pump if the distance is too large is the

A. vertical distance between pump and inlet
B. horizontal distance between pump and inlet
C. sloping distance between pump and inlet
D. horizontal distance from pump to outlet

25. A change in the slope of a vitrified pipe sewer should be located 25.____

    A. a few feet upstream from a manhole
    B. a few feet downstream from a manhole
    C. midway between manholes
    D. at a manhole

KEY (CORRECT ANSWERS)

1. C
2. B
3. B
4. A
5. C

6. A
7. C
8. A
9. B
10. D

11. A
12. D
13. D
14. C
15. B

16. B
17. B
18. B
19. C
20. B

21. C
22. D
23. A
24. A
25. D

TEST 2

DIRECTIONS: Each question or incomplete statement is followed by several suggested answers or completions. Select the one that BEST answers the question or completes the statement. *PRINT THE LETTER OF THE CORRECT ANSWER IN THE SPACE AT THE RIGHT.*

1. Box sheeting differs from regular sheeting PRIMARILY in   1.____

    A. size of timber used for sheeting
    B. that it is used in trenches of short length
    C. that it is used in trenches of greater width
    D. the direction in which the sheeting is placed

2. Assume that sewage is flowing out of three adjacent manholes on a sewer line. It is MOST logical to expect that there is an obstruction   2.____

    A. between the center manhole and the higher one
    B. between the center manhole and the lower one
    C. anywhere between the three manholes
    D. outside the stretch of sewer between the three manholes

3. Earth used to backfill a vitrified pipe sewer trench   3.____

    A. should not contain any stones
    B. may contain stones if the stones are less than 10 inches in largest dimension
    C. should contain only those stones removed from the trench
    D. may contain stones up to 10 inches in largest dimension provided there are no stones in the backfill which is within 2 feet of the pipe

4. When laying bell and spigot sewer pipe, it is GOOD practice to place the ball end   4.____

    A. away from the outlet
    B. toward the outlet
    C. either way
    D. away from the outlet when the sewer has a flat slope

5. The number of board feet in 22 pieces of 2 x 6's, 12'6" long is MOST NEARLY   5.____

    A. 275   B. 270   C. 265   D. 260

6. A riser would MOST likely be used on a _____ sewer.   6.____

    A. shallow   B. vitrified pipe
    C. deep   D. reinforced concrete pipe

7. If, after ramming, a granite block is found to be too low, it should be   7.____

    A. replaced with a thicker block
    B. removed with a pinch bar
    C. covered with mortar
    D. removed with tongs

8. A separating agent, such as calcium chloride, would MOST likely be used on a(n) _____ pavement with _____ filler.   8.____

A. granite block; cement grout
B. asphalt block; cement grout joint
C. granite block; asphaltic joint
D. poured concrete; cement grout joint

9. Assume that granite block has been redressed.
   The dimension which is MOST likely to be the same as that on the original block is

   A. length   B. width   C. depth   D. none

10. Spacing strips are MOST likely to be used when laying _____ block pavement with _____ joint filler.

    A. asphalt; cement grout   B. asphalt; asphaltic
    C. granite; cement grout   D. granite; asphaltic

11. The piece of equipment MOST likely to be used both for sheet asphalt pavement and asphalt block pavement is a(n)

    A. tamper   B. smoothing iron
    C. asphalt rake   D. asphalt kettle

12. In cleaning a steel reinforcing bar for reinforced concrete, it is LEAST important to remove

    A. rust   B. grease   C. oil   D. paint

13. Concrete that is used for a concrete base for pavement should have a slump of MOST NEARLY _____ inches.

    A. 10   B. 8   C. 6   D. 3

14. A concrete mix can be made more workable without reducing its strength by adding to the mix

    A. cement   B. water
    C. cement and water   D. coarse aggregate

15. Forms for concrete are usually oiled to

    A. prevent honeycombing
    B. make the form watertight
    C. prevent segregation
    D. make stripping easier

16. The backlash in a roller used on sheet asphalt is

    A. *good,* because it makes for faster operation
    B. *good,* because it makes the operator's job easier
    C. *bad,* because it results in waves in the asphalt
    D. *bad,* because it requires more asphaltic cement

17. The LARGEST particles in the binder course of a sheet asphalt pavement usually consists of

    A. broken stone   B. sand
    C. smooth round pebbles   D. rock dust

18. It is important to remove water which has seeped into bell holes in a sewer trench because

   A. this makes the caulker more comfortable
   B. this water will spoil the joint
   C. this water will preserve the stability of the trench bottom
   D. the water is unsanitary

19. Of the following materials, the one which would be MOST combustible is _____ asphalt.

   A. RG cutback
   B. MC cutback
   C. SC cutback
   D. emulsified

20. The one and one-half inch stones of a base for an asphalt macadam pavement have been rolled.
    The BEST time to apply the asphalt cement is

   A. immediately after the rolling
   B. after the rolled stones have been wet down with water
   C. after sand has been spread over the broken stone
   D. after sand has been spread and rolled

21. The binder course of a sheet asphalt pavement has been laid today. The surface course should be placed

   A. today
   B. tomorrow
   C. the day after tomorrow
   D. any day next week

Questions 22-23.

DIRECTIONS: Questions 22 and 23 refer to a 12-inch sewer line which is being constructed without a cradle in a clay soil.

22. Before the pipe is placed in the trench, the bottom of the trench should be excavated to a depth of MOST NEARLY _____ inches _____ the invert.

   A. 12; below
   B. 6; below
   C. 12; above
   D. 6; above

23. After the pipe is properly bedded, the excavated material should be replaced in layers

   A. 6 inches thick, each layer being flooded with water
   B. 6 inches thick, each layer being tamped
   C. 4 feet thick, each layer being tamped
   D. 2 feet thick, each layer being flooded with water

24. In sewer work, pargeting would MOST likely be required on

   A. vitrified pipe sewers
   B. manholes
   C. cast iron pipe sewers
   D. reinforced concrete pipe sewers

25. A seal coat for an asphalt macadam base course has been applied by a pressure distributor.
Before a seal coat is rolled, it should be

    A. allowed to cool
    B. covered with broken stone
    C. wet down with water
    D. squeegeed over the surface

KEY (CORRECT ANSWERS)

1.	D	11.	D
2.	D	12.	A
3.	D	13.	D
4.	A	14.	C
5.	A	15.	D
6.	C	16.	C
7.	D	17.	A
8.	C	18.	B
9.	C	19.	A
10.	A	20.	A

21. A
22. B
23. B
24. B
25. B

EXAMINATION SECTION
TEST 1

DIRECTIONS: Each question or incomplete statement is followed by several suggested answers or completions. Select the one that BEST answers the question or completes the statement. *PRINT THE LETTER OF THE CORRECT ANSWER IN THE SPACE AT THE RIGHT.*

1. Before placing asphalt block for a pavement on the concrete base, the concrete base should be

    A. wet down with water
    B. painted with hot asphaltic cement
    C. covered with a bitumen-sand bed
    D. covered with broken stone

2. Of the following ingredients, the one which is present in asphaltic concrete but not in a sheet asphalt mix is

    A. asphaltic cement   B. sand
    C. mineral dust   D. broken stone

3. Of the following materials, the one which would make the BEST macadam base course is

    A. freshly broken rock consisting of angular pieces
    B. broken rock which had weathered for a long time
    C. gravel consisting of smooth round rock
    D. freshly crushed gravel

4. The one of the following in which a surface heater would be MOST useful is

    A. new concrete construction
    B. new asphalt construction
    C. repair work on concrete
    D. repair work on asphalt

5. A pneumatic jack hammer is powered by

    A. compressed air   B. electricity
    C. steam   D. water pressure

6. A mattock could be BEST used in place of a

    A. hammer   B. pick-axe   C. rake   D. shovel

7. The one of the following tools that is used to finish concrete so that a very smooth surface is obtained is

    A. template   B. trowel
    C. vibrator   D. wooden float

8. The type of cement used in MOST concrete work is called

    A. asbestos   B. natural   C. Portland   D. rock

9. Cement brought on the job in bags should be

   A. piled in criss-cross stacks on the ground near the work
   B. piled in stacks 10 bags high in a convenient place on the ground
   C. put on a platform and covered with waterproof covering
   D. put under a tree or awning where the sun's rays can't reach it

10. In the concrete trade, sand is called

    A. binder
    B. coarse aggregate
    C. filler
    D. fine aggregate

11. A 1:2:4 concrete mix means one part _____, two parts _____, four parts _____.

    A. cement; gravel; sand
    B. cement; sand; gravel
    C. gravel; sand; cement
    D. sand; gravel; cement

12. A slump test is used in concrete to determine

    A. consistency
    B. construction
    C. expansion
    D. slope

13. After mixing, the *initial* set of concrete will take place in about _____ hour(s).

    A. 3/4 of an
    B. 2 1/4
    C. 4 3/4
    D. 8

14. Concrete that has become partly set in the mixer should be

    A. covered with water for about 24 hours to soften it before using
    B. discarded and not used at all
    C. mixed in with another regular batch of concrete before using
    D. re-tempered by adding more cement and mixed again before using

15. In hot weather, newly-placed concrete will set better when it is

    A. covered with wet burlap
    B. dried by exposure to the sun
    C. mixed with grout
    D. shaded from the sun's rays

16. A 1:2:4 concrete mix is prepared on the job with 10 gallons of water. This concrete mix is

    A. *desirable,* because it will require less tamping
    B. *desirable,* because it will set faster
    C. *undesirable,* because its strength is reduced by excess water
    D. *undesirable,* because it will show less honeycomb

17. Of the following, the one which will lengthen the setting time of concrete is a(n)

    A. higher water temperature
    B. increase in proportion of water used
    C. less humid atmosphere
    D. shorter mixing period

18. Of the following, quick drying of concrete will MOST likely cause

    A. air bubbles B. bumps
    C. cracks   D. swelling

19. Of the following, the BEST way to prepare an old concrete surface for a new layer of concrete is to

    A. clean it and apply a rich cement mortar
    B. cover it with wet sand
    C. steam and dry it
    D. wash it thoroughly and leave it wet

20. Grout is used MAINLY to

    A. fill surface impressions and imperfections
    B. lower the freezing point of the concrete mix
    C. make the base harden faster
    D. provide a wearing surface layer

21. The usual method of repairing cracks in concrete roadways is to fill with

    A. limestone   B. mineral filler
    C. sand   D. tar

22. Joints are placed in concrete sidewalks to take care of

    A. bumps   B. cracks
    C. drainage   D. expansion and contraction

23. To take care of surface drainage, concrete sidewalks usually have slopes of _____ inch(es) to the foot.

    A. 1/4   B. 1   C. 2   D. 3

24. The grade of a street is the

    A. AAA rating of the street's riding qualities
    B. difference in height between the crown and berm
    C. slope of a cut or fill
    D. variation in elevation per 100 feet

25. If a street rises 2' in 400', the grade is

    A. 0.2%   B. 0.5%   C. 2.0%   D. 5.0%

KEY (CORRECT ANSWERS)

1. C
2. D
3. A
4. D
5. A

6. B
7. B
8. C
9. C
10. D

11. B
12. A
13. A
14. B
15. A

16. C
17. B
18. C
19. A
20. A

21. D
22. D
23. A
24. D
25. B

TEST 2

DIRECTIONS: Each question or incomplete statement is followed by several suggested answers or completions. Select the one that BEST answers the question or completes the statement. *PRINT THE LETTER OF THE CORRECT ANSWER IN THE SPACE AT THE RIGHT.*

1. The top course of an asphalt pavement is known as the _____ course.

    A. aggregate   B. base   C. binder   D. wearing

    1._____

2. In paving terms, a two-course concrete sidewalk is one which is

    A. composed of concrete both hand and machine mixed
    B. composed of two layers, a base and a wearing surface
    C. wide enough for traffic going in opposite directions
    D. wide enough for two pedestrians to walk side by side

    2._____

3. The foundations for asphalt surface should be

    A. clean and damp
    B. clean and dry
    C. damp and sprinkled with sand
    D. dry and sprinkled with sand

    3._____

4. A catch basin is used to

    A. detain floating rubbish which might clog a sewer
    B. hold water used in flushing sewers
    C. record and measure the depth of flow of sewage
    D. regulate the flow of sewage to a treatment plant

    4._____

5. A sewer built to carry the flows in excess of the capacity of an existing sewer is called a _____ sewer.

    A. lateral   B. main   C. relief   D. trunk

    5._____

6. A sewer designed to carry domestic sewage, industrial waste, and storm sewage is called a

    A. combined sewer   B. house connection
    C. sanitary sewer   D. storm sewer

    6._____

7. A pipe conveying sewage from a single building to a common sewer is called a

    A. catch basin   B. grease trap
    C. house connection   D. relief sewer

    7._____

8. The PRINCIPAL effort in maintaining sewers is to keep them

    A. clean and unobstructed
    B. free from poisonous gases
    C. free of illegal connections
    D. properly backfilled

    8._____

9. Catch basins in unpaved streets should be cleaned

   A. daily in winter, weekly in summer
   B. once a year
   C. every six months
   D. after every large storm

10. In using a flexible sewer rod to clean a sewer, the work is usually begun at the

    A. chimney between manholes
    B. nearest catch basin
    C. top of the flooded manhole
    D. nearest house connection

11. In flushing sewers, the MOST important of the following qualities of the water used is its

    A. cleanliness   B. quantity
    C. temperature   D. velocity

12. Grease can be prevented from entering a sewer by the

    A. addition of copper sulfate
    B. installation of a copper ring in pipe joints
    C. installation of a separator
    D. coating of the outside of the pipe with tar

13. Manholes are used CHIEFLY as a(n)

    A. access for cleaning sewers
    B. outlet for sewer gas
    C. run-off for storm water
    D. support for sewer pipes

14. If the sewage at a manhole is backed up, it indicates MOST probably that, with respect to this manhole, there is an obstruction in the

    A. nearest catch basin   B. nearest house connection
    C. upstream sewer   D. downstream sewer

15. The one of the following at which a manhole in a sewer line is NOT necessary is wherever there is a

    A. change in direction
    B. change in pipe size
    C. considerable change in grade
    D. house connection

16. Manholes are usually placed at intervals of _____ to _____ feet.

    A. 50; 75   B. 100; 200   C. 700; 900   D. 1200; 1400

17. Of the following, the STRONGEST method for sheeting a trench is

    A. box sheeting   B. poling boards
    C. stay bracing   D. vertical sheeting

18. The one of the following that would be MOST commonly used to join a house sewer to a common sewer is a(n) 18.____

    A. increaser
    B. reducer
    C. running trap
    D. Y branch

19. After making joints in sewer pipe, the minimum safe length of time to allow before they should be exposed to running water is _____ hour(s). 19.____

    A. 1
    B. 8
    C. 24
    D. 48

20. The one of the following that is the LEAST important health precaution for a sewer worker to take is 20.____

    A. frequent washing
    B. shading his eyes from reflected light
    C. using an antiseptic in cuts
    D. wearing rubber gloves

Questions 21-25.

DIRECTIONS: Column I below contains pictures of pipe connections used in sewer lines. Column II lists the names of these fittings. For each picture, indicate the capital letter preceding its correct name in Column II.

21.

COLUMN II 21.____

A. Elbow
B. Reducer
C. Running trap
D. T branch
E. Y branch

22. 22.____

23. 23.____

4 (#2)

24.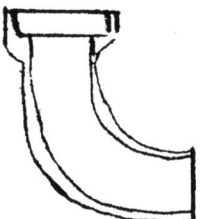

24.____

25.

25.____

KEY (CORRECT ANSWERS)

1. D
2. B
3. B
4. A
5. C

6. A
7. C
8. A
9. D
10. C

11. D
12. C
13. A
14. D
15. D

16. A
17. D
18. D
19. C
20. B

21. E
22. D
23. C
24. A
25. B

EXAMINATION SECTION
TEST 1

DIRECTIONS: Each question or incomplete statement is followed by several suggested answers or completions. Select the one that BEST answers the question or completes the statement. *PRINT THE LETTER OF THE CORRECT ANSWER IN THE SPACE AT THE RIGHT.*

1. Of the following statements relating to new bell and spigot pipe being laid in a trench, the one that is CORRECT is that

   A. the enlarged end of the pipe faces downstream
   B. bell and spigot pipe is usually elliptical in shape
   C. when building a new line using bell and spigot pipe, you start from the downstream end
   D. vitrified pipe is usually thicker than concrete pipe of the same diameter

   1.____

2. Vitrified pipe is made of

   A. clay
   B. vermiculite
   C. gypsum
   D. Portland cement

   2.____

3. The invert of a sewer pipe is its

   A. outer top
   B. inner bottom
   C. inner top
   D. outer bottom

   3.____

4. A cradle is usually placed under a sewer pipe when the

   A. trench is narrow
   B. trench is wide
   C. soil is poor
   D. pipe is near the surface

   4.____

5. A monolithic sewer is a

   A. vitrified pipe sewer
   B. sewer carrying only storm water
   C. cast-iron sewer containing bell and spigot joints
   D. reinforced concrete cast-in-place sewer

   5.____

6. Of the following, the BEST reason for placing manholes on sewers is to

   A. provide access for inspection and maintenance
   B. allow for overflow during a heavy storm
   C. pinpoint the location of the sewer
   D. give access to the sewer for the purpose of snow removal

   6.____

7. The sheeting in a trench for a sheeted sewer is ordered left in place after the sewer has been built and backfilled. The BEST reason for ordering the sheeting left in place is that

   A. the sheeting is too expensive to remove
   B. the removal of the sheeting would disturb the sewer
   C. this minimizes the settlement outside the sheeted area
   D. the sheeting is too difficult to remove

   7.____

8. The two MOST frequently used types of sheeting for normal soil conditions and average depths are

   A. soldier beams with horizontal sheeting and vertical wood sheeting with bracing
   B. steel sheet piling and vertical wood sheeting
   C. precast concrete planks with soldier beams and steel sheet piling
   D. slurry walls and vertical wood sheeting

9. A specification for a new sewer requires that the pavement NOT be restored for a period of at least six months after the backfill is in place.
   The BEST reason for this requirement is to

   A. be sure that the sewer will work before restoring the pavement
   B. minimize the settlement of the pavement
   C. defer final payment to the contractor
   D. allow the use of a lighter pavement

10. In reinforced concrete sewers, the reinforcing steel must have a minimum cover of concrete.
    Of the following, the BEST reason for this requirement is to

    A. make the sewer watertight
    B. protect the reinforcing steel against corrosion
    C. allow the use of smaller sized stone in the concrete
    D. eliminate the need for vibrating concrete

11. As used in relation to sewers, infiltration refers to the

    A. leakage of sewage from the sewer to the surrounding soil
    B. connection of sanitary sewer lines into storm water sewers
    C. inflow of ground water into the sewer
    D. loss of mortar at the joints of prefabricated sewers

12. A BAD effect of infiltration in a sanitary sewer is that it

    A. tends to overload the sewage treatment plant
    B. corrodes the sewer
    C. causes cavitation in the sewer
    D. increases the carrying capacity of the sewer

13. A storm sewer GENERALLY differs from a sanitary sewer in that a storm sewer

    A. is generally larger in size than a sanitary sewer and carries little dry-weather flow
    B. is generally made of concrete whereas a sanitary sewer is generally made of cast iron
    C. generally requires fewer manholes than a sanitary sewer
    D. generally has a large slope whereas a sanitary sewer generally has a small slope

14. Manhole frames and covers are USUALLY made of

    A. aluminum   B. malleable iron
    C. cast iron   D. steel

15. The spacing of rungs used for steps in a manhole is MOST NEARLY _____ inches. 15.____
    A. 4   B. 12   C. 20   D. 26

16. Steel is galvanized by coating it with 16.____
    A. tin   B. lead   C. copper   D. zinc

17. The reinforcing steel in a cast-in-place concrete sewer section would MOST likely be placed as shown in 17.____

    A.   B.

    C.   D.

18. Well points would MOST likely be used in the construction of a sewer when the 18.____
    A. sewer is very deep
    B. sewer is in rock
    C. soil is clayey
    D. water table is above the sewer

19. The purpose of jetting the well points in sewer construction is to 19.____
    A. clean out the screen
    B. set the well point in place
    C. clean out the area outside the screen
    D. remove water from the surrounding area

20. The type of soil in which well points operate MOST efficiently is 20.____
    A. sand   B. clay   C. rock   D. silt

21. The water-cement ratio of a concrete mix is USUALLY expressed in terms of 21.____
    A. barrels of cement per gallon of water
    B. bags of cement per gallon of water
    C. gallons of water per bag of cement
    D. gallons of water per barrel of cement

22. The effective diameter of a number 4 reinforcing bar is MOST NEARLY _____ inch.

    A. 1/4   B. 1/2   C. 3/4   D. 1

23. The PRIMARY purpose of curing freshly poured concrete is to

    A. keep the surface smooth
    B. prevent honeycombing of the surface
    C. improve the appearance of the surface
    D. prevent evaporation of water from the surface

24. A bag of cement weighs MOST NEARLY _____ pounds.

    A. 94   B. 104   C. 114   D. 124

25. Of the following, the material that may be used as the coarse aggregate in ordinary Portland cement concrete is

    A. well graded sand
    B. sand of uniform size
    C. crushed rock
    D. micaschist

26. In a 1:2:4 concrete mix, the 2 stands for the quantity of

    A. water
    B. fine aggregate
    C. coarse aggregate
    D. cement

27. The height of a slump cone used in concrete testing is _____ inches.

    A. 6   B. 8   C. 10   D. 12

28. As commonly used, 3000-pound concrete refers to 3000 pounds per

    A. inch
    B. square inch
    C. cubic inch
    D. foot

29. The factor that has the GREATEST effect on the strength of concrete is the

    A. size of coarse aggregate
    B. uniformity of the aggregate
    C. water-cement ratio
    D. quality of the fine aggregate

30. The number of bags of cement needed to produce a cubic yard of concrete is called the _____ factor.

    A. cement   B. yield   C. bulk   D. output

31. The MAIN purpose of vibrating newly poured concrete when it is in the forms is to

    A. remove high points on the surface
    B. eliminate air pockets on the surface
    C. remove excess water
    D. distribute the aggregate evenly in the concrete

32. A cubic foot of ordinary Portland cement concrete weighs MOST NEARLY _____ pounds.

    A. 145   B. 165   C. 195   D. 220

33. The MAIN purpose of adding an air entraining agent to a concrete mix used for sidewalks is to 33.____

    A. improve the resistance of the concrete to freezing and thawing conditions
    B. decrease the weight of the concrete to lighten the dead load of the concrete
    C. increase the compressive strength of the concrete
    D. decrease the resistance of the concrete to bleeding

34. Of the following operations on a fresh concrete surface, the one that should be performed FIRST is 34.____

    A. screeding   B. floating
    C. trowelling   D. brooming

35. When concrete is referred to as *3000-pound concrete*, the *3000* refers to its strength at the end of _____ days. 35.____

    A. 7   B. 14   C. 21   D. 28

KEY (CORRECT ANSWERS)

1. C		16. D	
2. A		17. A	
3. B		18. D	
4. C		19. B	
5. D		20. A	
6. A		21. C	
7. C		22. B	
8. A		23. D	
9. B		24. A	
10. B		25. C	
11. C		26. B	
12. A		27. D	
13. A		28. B	
14. C		29. C	
15. B		30. A	

31. B
32. A
33. A
34. A
35. D

TEST 2

DIRECTIONS: Each question or incomplete statement is followed by several suggested answers or completions. Select the one that BEST answers the question or completes the statement. *PRINT THE LETTER OF THE CORRECT ANSWER IN THE SPACE AT THE RIGHT.*

1. If a batch of concrete is very stiff, its MAIN characteristic is that it 1.____

   A. has a low slump B. has a high slump
   C. is undersanded D. is oversanded

2. Reinforcing steel should have the GREATEST cover of concrete when the concrete surface is 2.____

   A. in contact with the ground
   B. in contact with outside air
   C. an interior wall
   D. an interior ceiling

3. The MAIN difference between reinforced concrete and plain concrete is that plain concrete uses _____ for reinforcing. 3.____

   A. larger aggregate
   B. high early strength cement
   C. steel
   D. a low water-cement ratio

4. Of the following types of wood, the one that would MOST likely be used in form work for concrete is 4.____

   A. oak   B. maple   C. fir   D. birch

5. The size that SEPARATES the fine aggregate from the coarse aggregate in a concrete mix is _____ inch. 5.____

   A. 1/8   B. 1/4   C. 3/8   D. 1/2

6. The MINIMUM thickness of sidewalk pavements for pedes-trian use should be _____ inches. 6.____

   A. 4   B. 5   C. 6   D. 7

7. An ADVANTAGE of using sand instead of salt on concrete roadway surfaces when snow and ice settle on them is that sand 7.____

   A. is easier to remove than salt when the snow disappears
   B. will harm catch basins less than salt when the materials are washed into the catch basin
   C. will not harm the concrete surface whereas salt is harmful to the surface
   D. will help melt the surface ice whereas salt will have no effect on the ice on the surface

8. Sidewalks should be pitched toward the street at a MINIMUM of _____ inch per _____.

   A. 1/8; foot
   B. 1/8; yard
   C. 5/8; foot
   D. 1; foot

9. A freshly poured concrete sidewalk is usually finished with a

   A. screed
   B. wood float
   C. steel trowel
   D. darby

10. Roadway

    The shape of the roadway section shown above is USUALLY a(n)

    A. circle   B. ellipse   C. parabola   D. hyperbola

11. The MAIN advantage of using large coarse aggregate in a concrete mix is that

    A. the mix is more workable
    B. the mix is stronger
    C. there is a saving in cement
    D. less water is required

12. In building a new street, sidewalk, and curb in a previously unpaved area, the order of construction practically ALWAYS followed is that the

    A. sidewalk precedes the road pavement
    B. sidewalk follows the road pavement
    C. curb precedes the road pavement
    D. road pavement precedes the curb

13. The USUAL range of depth of a curb from top surface of road at curb to top of curb is _____ inches to _____ inches.

    A. 4; 8   B. 8; 12   C. 12; 16   D. 16; 20

14. The dimensions of common brick are GENERALLY

    A. 2 1/4" x 2 3/4" x 12"
    B. 2 1/4" x 3 3/4" x 8"
    C. 2 3/4" x 3 3/4" x 8"
    D. 2 3/4" x 4 3/4" x 12"

15. Common brick is made of

    A. limestone   B. sand   C. clay   D. loess

16. Carbon black is added to concrete to

    A. give the concrete a black color
    B. accelerate the setting of the concrete
    C. retard the setting of the concrete
    D. improve the workability of the concrete

17. When steel curb angles are used for curbs, anchors are attached, to the curb angles. The MAIN purpose of the anchors is to

    A. hold the curb in place when the curb is being poured
    B. bond the curb angle into the concrete curb
    C. anchor the curb angle into the soil
    D. anchor the curb angle into the sidewalk

17.____

18. Wire mesh is specified in pounds per

    A. square foot
    B. square yard
    C. hundred square feet
    D. hundred square yards

18.____

19.

    An asphalt pavement consists of three layers.
    The layer marked E in the sketch above is the _____ course.

    A. tack   B. binder   C. base   D. wearing

19.____

20. The BASE course of a sheet asphalt pavement is usually made of

    A. sheet asphalt
    B. concrete
    C. tar
    D. bituminous binder

20.____

21. In asphalt paving, the tack coat is USUALLY applied

    A. on the finished wearing surface
    B. on the surface of the soil to receive the pavement
    C. on hard dense impervious surfaces
    D. along the curb

21.____

22. The specification for a pavement states that the penetration of asphalt is measured in units of mm.
    This stands for

    A. micrometer
    B. macrometer
    C. manometer
    D. millimeter

22.____

23. In an asphalt pavement, the LIQUID part of the asphalt mix is

    A. bitumen   B. water   C. gasoline   D. benzene

23.____

24. The terms liquid limit, plastic limit, and plasticity index refer to tests on

    A. asphalt   B. soil   C. concrete   D. gravel

24.____

25. For a bituminous paving material, sieves and sieve analysis are used to analyze the

    A. cement   B. aggregate   C. clay   D. silt

25.____

26. The size of sidewalk panels is USUALLY

    A. 2' x 2'   B. 3' x 3'   C. 5' x 5'   D. 6' x 6'

26.____

27. The slope of a sidewalk is designated as 2 inches in 5 feet.
    The drop in elevation of the sidewalk in 30' is _____ foot.

    A. one   B. 1/2 of a   C. 3/4 of a   D. 1/4 of a

28. In placing temporary asphaltic pavement upon completion of the backfill in a street opening, a 3 inch thick pavement should be laid one inch above the adjoining asphalt permanent pavement.
    The MAIN reason for making the temporary pavement one inch above the finished pavement is to

    A. provide adequate drainage
    B. allow for settlement
    C. identify the temporarily paved area
    D. save excavation when the permanent pavement is placed

29. A maintenance bond for a roadway pavement is in an amount of 10% of the estimated cost.
    If the estimated cost is $80,000, the maintenance bond is

    A. $80   B. $800   C. $8,000   D. $80,000

30. Specifications require that a core be taken every 700 square yards of paved roadway or fraction thereof.
    A 100 foot by 200 foot rectangular area would require _____ core(s).

    A. 1   B. 2   C. 3   D. 4

31. An applicant must file a map at a scale of 1" = 40'.
    Six inches on the map represents _____ feet on the ground.

    A. 600   B. 240   C. 120   D. D, 60

32. A 100' x 110' lot has an area of MOST NEARLY _____ acre.

    A. 1/8   B. 1/4   C. 3/8   D. 1/2

33. 1 inch is MOST NEARLY equal to _____ feet.

    A. .02   B. .04   C. .06   D. .08

34. The area of the triangle EFG shown at the right is MOST NEARLY _____ sq.ft.
    A. 36
    B. 42
    C. 48
    D. 54

35. Specifications state: As further security for the faith-ful performance of this contract, the comptroller shall deduct, and retain until the final payment, 10% of the value of the work certified for payment in each partial payment voucher, until the amount so deducted and retained shall equal 5% of the contract price or in the case of a unit price contract, 5% of the estimated amount to be paid to the contractor under the contract.
    For a $300,000 contract, the amount to be retained at the end of the contract is

    A. $5,000   B. $10,000   C. $15,000   D. $20,000

KEY (CORRECT ANSWERS)

1.	A	16.	A
2.	A	17.	B
3.	A	18.	C
4.	C	19.	B
5.	B	20.	B
6.	A	21.	C
7.	C	22.	D
8.	A	23.	A
9.	B	24.	B
10.	C	25.	B
11.	C	26.	C
12.	C	27.	A
13.	A	28.	B
14.	B	29.	C
15.	C	30.	D

31. B
32. B
33. D
34. A
35. C

TEST 3

DIRECTIONS: Each question or incomplete statement is followed by several suggested answers or completions. Select the one that BEST answers the question or completes the statement. *PRINT THE LETTER OF THE CORRECT ANSWER IN THE SPACE AT THE RIGHT.*

Questions 1-4.

DIRECTIONS: Questions 1 through 4, inclusive, refer to the plan of a sewer shown below.

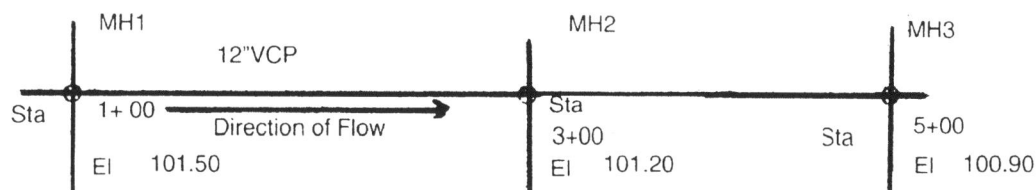

PLAN - SEWER

1. The distance, in feet, between MH1 and MH3 is _____ feet.   1.____

    A. 200   B. 300   C. 400   D. 500

2. The drop in elevation between MH1 and MH3 is   2.____

    A. 0.60'   B. 0.50'   C. 0.40'   D. 0.30'

3. If the scale of the drawing is 1 inch = 40 feet, the length of the line on the plan between MH1 and MH2 should be, in inches,   3.____

    A. 3   B. 4   C. 5   D. 6

4. A vertical section taken along the length of the sewer would be called a   4.____

    A. cross section   B. development
    C. partial plan   D. profile

5. A line joining points of equal elevation on a plan is known as a(n)   5.____

    A. profile   B. contour   C. elevation   D. isobar

6. The Federal agency concerned with safety on a construction site is   6.____

    A. OSHA   B. FIDC   C. FEMA   D. NHOC

7. A Federal safety requirement on construction sites is that   7.____

    A. a nurse must be present at all times
    B. a safety inspector, whose only duty is safety, be assigned full time to construction sites
    C. safety hats must be worn
    D. metal scaffolds are not permitted on the job site

37

8. Safety shoes are shoes that have a(n)

   A. extra heavy sole
   B. extra heavy heel
   C. metal covering the toe
   D. special leather covering over the ankles

9. A material whose use has been curtailed in building and heavy construction is

   A. poured cut asphalt
   B. lightweight concrete aggregate
   C. latex paint
   D. sprayed-on asbestos

10. In making a field report, it is POOR practice to erase information on the report in order to make a change because

    A. there is a question of what was changed and why it was changed
    B. you are liable to erase through the paper and tear the report
    C. the report will no longer look neat and presentable
    D. the duplicate copies will be smudged

11. It is PREFERABLE to print information on a field report rather than write it out longhand mainly because

    A. printing takes less time to write than writing long-hand
    B. printing is usually easier to read than longhand writing
    C. longhand writing on field reports is not acceptable in court cases
    D. printing occupies less space on a report than long hand writing

12. Where the length of roadway pavement is less than 100 lineal feet, the requirement of cores may be waived.
    The term waived in the above statement means MOST NEARLY

    A. eliminated   B. enforced
    C. considered   D. postponed

13. Inspectors are provided with standardized forms, and they have to fill in information as requested on the form.
    Of the following, the MAIN advantage of this type of form is that

    A. the inspector will be less likely to omit important information
    B. it is cheap to print
    C. it is confidential and only authorized people will see it
    D. it is easy to make copies of the form

14. Where only part of the sidewalk is to be relaid, the concrete shall match the predominant color of the existing sidewalk.
    The word predominant in the above sentence means MOST NEARLY

    A. lightest   B. darkest
    C. main   D. contrasting

15. All stands must be substantially built so as not to create any hazard to passersby or other persons.
    The word hazard in the above sentence means MOST NEARLY

    A. delay B. danger
    C. obstruction D. inconvenience

16. The lights shall be lighted and remain lighted every night during the hours prescribed for public street lamps.
    The word prescribed in the above sentence means MOST NEARLY

    A. required B. not needed
    C. before midnight D. of darkness

17. The Department of Highways in its discretion may direct that certain regulations be waived.
    In the above sentence, the word discretion means MOST NEARLY

    A. jurisdiction B. operation
    C. organization D. judgment

18. A sidewalk that abuts a curb _____ the curb.

    A. is above B. is below
    C. touches D. is integral with

19. All canopy permits shall be posted in a conspicuous place at the entrance for which the permit is issued.
    The word conspicuous means MOST NEARLY

    A. well known B. inaccessible
    C. easily observed D. obscure

20. Where a street opening is made by a licensed plumber, a plunber's bond may be filed in lieu of a street obstruction bond.
    The words in lieu of mean MOST NEARLY

    A. in addition to B. instead of
    C. immediately as D. appurtenant to

21. Of the following characteristics of a written report, the one that is MOST important is its

    A. length B. accuracy
    C. organization D. grammar

22. A written report to your superior contains many spelling errors.
    Of the following statements relating to spelling errors, the one that is MOST NEARLY correct is that

    A. this is unimportant as long as the meaning of the report is clear
    B. readers of the report will ignore the many spelling errors
    C. readers of the report will get a poor opinion of the writer of the report
    D. spelling errors are unimportant as long as the grammar is correct

23. Written reports to your superior should have the same general arrangement and layout. 23.____
    The BEST reason for this requirement is that the

    A. report will be more accurate
    B. report will be more complete
    C. person who reads the report will know what the subject of the report is
    D. person who reads the report will know where to look for information in the report

24. The first paragraph of a report usually contains detailed information on the subject of the 24.____
    report.
    Of the following, the BEST reason for this requirement is to enable the

    A. reader to quickly find the subject of the report
    B. typist to immediately determine the subject of the report so that she will understand what she is typing
    C. clerk to determine to whom copies of the report shall be routed
    D. typist to quickly determine how many copies of the report will be needed

Questions 25-26.

DIRECTIONS: Questions 25 and 26 refer to the girder shown in the sketch below.

25. A report speaks of stiffeners on girders. 25.____
    The stiffener would be the part shown as

    A. A   B. B   C. C   D. D

26. The flange would be the part shown as 26.____

    A. E   B. B   C. C   D. D

27. When an inspector is writing a report about a problem your agency handles, the report 27.____
    should contain four major parts: a description of the problem, the location, the details of
    the problem, and

    A. your recommendation
    B. references to the drawings that pertain to the problem
    C. the borough in which the problem is located
    D. the agency to whom the problem should be referred

28. A report refers to a Pratt truss. 28.____
    The material composition of the truss is MOST likely

    A. wood   B. concrete   C. steel   D. aluminum

29. A plumb bob is USUALLY used to

   A. check grades
   B. establish a vertical line
   C. hold down equipment
   D. check the grading of sand

30. As a general rule, any time a measurement is made in the field, the number of quantity should be immediately recorded.
    Of the following, the BEST reason for immediately recording this information is that

   A. the office is interested in receiving this information as quickly as possible
   B. this enables the inspector to complete his report more quickly
   C. this information may be needed for computations
   D. it is easy to forget or mistake numbers if they are not immediately recorded

---

KEY(CORRECT ANSWERS)

1.	C	16.	A
2.	A	17.	D
3.	C	18.	C
4.	D	19.	C
5.	B	20.	B
6.	A	21.	B
7.	C	22.	C
8.	C	23.	D
9.	D	24.	A
10.	A	25.	D
11.	B	26.	B
12.	A	27.	A
13.	A	28.	C
14.	C	29.	B
15.	B	30.	D

EXAMINATION SECTION
TEST 1

DIRECTIONS: Each question or incomplete statement is followed by several suggested answers or completions. Select the one that BEST answers the question or completes the statement. *PRINT THE LETTER OF THE CORRECT ANSWER IN THE SPACE AT THE RIGHT.*

1. If cast iron weighs 450 pounds per cubic foot, the weight of a solid cast iron manhole cover 2 feet in diameter and 1 inch thick is MOST NEARLY _____ pounds.

    A. 94 B. 118 C. 136 D. 164

2. A gas which has an odor similar to rotten eggs is

    A. argon
    B. phosgene
    C. nitrogen
    D. hydrogen sulfide

3. The gases released by digesting sewage sludges contain about 72%

    A. methane B. chlorine C. helium D. copper

4. In sewer maintenance, an orange peel bucket is USUALLY used for

    A. testing for toxic gases
    B. rodding sewers
    C. cleaning roof drains
    D. cleaning catch basins

5. A plumbing device that prevents the passage of bad odors and gases from the sewer system to a building is a

    A. corporation stop
    B. union
    C. curb box
    D. trap

6. An 8-inch diameter sewer enters at the upstream side of a manhole, and a 10-inch sewer leaves at the downstream side. The crowns of the sewers are at the same elevation. If the invert elevation of the 8-inch sewer is 100.64 feet, the invert elevation of the 10-inch sewer is MOST NEARLY _____ feet.

    A. 100.32 B. 100.41 C. 100.47 D. 100.52

7. Where ground slopes are unfavorable, it is necessary to keep sanitary sewer grades at the minimum velocity that will prevent the settling of material when the sewer is flowing full.
The velocity is MOST NEARLY _____ feet per second.

    A. 0.2 B. 2.0 C. 20.0 D. 200.0

8. A condition that will permit polluted water to enter a potable water supply is a

    A. tide gate
    B. cross connection
    C. cathodic protection
    D. reducer

9. A wheel with a grooved rim such as is mounted in a pulley block to guide rope or cable is a

    A. turnbuckle
    B. wormgear
    C. slant
    D. sheave

10. A device used in a combined sewer to bypass excess storm-flow is a(n)

    A. soffit
    B. side-flow weir
    C. aquafer
    D. cellular cofferdam

11. A device installed at the discharge end of a sewer outfall which operates to permit gravity flow at low stages in the receiving waters, but closes to prevent backflow when the elevation of the receiving waters is high is a

    A. flume
    B. buttress
    C. tide gate
    D. flocculator

12. A pipe used to carry streamflow under a highway embankment is a

    A. culvert
    B. lock
    C. standpipe
    D. pitot

13. The pipe on the discharge side of a sewage pump is a

    A. tell-tale pipe
    B. sump pipe
    C. suction pipe
    D. force main

14. A model 6520 sewer cleaner is rated at 60 GPM at 1000 PSI. As used here, PSI is an abbreviation for

    A. positive surging inflow
    B. per sewer invert
    C. pounds per square inch
    D. pounds per sewer inlet

15. In order to increase culvert efficiency and to prevent undermining of the culvert, the entrance to the culvert is FREQUENTLY provided with a

    A. sump pump
    B. mud valve
    C. head wall
    D. scroll case

16. A sewer plan calls for pipe diameters of 3", 10", 12", 14", 15", and 18". The size which is NOT used for a standard strength clay sewer pipe is

    A. 10"
    B. 12"
    C. 14"
    D. 15"

17. Lateral sanitary sewers should PREFERABLY intersect at a

    A. catch basin
    B. weir
    C. manhole
    D. tide gate

18. A dip, or sag, used in a sewer line to pass under structures, such as subways, is called a(n)

    A. outfall
    B. inverted siphon
    C. force main
    D. regulator

19. A device suitable for pumping sewage from deep basements into city sewers is a

    A. pressure relief valve
    B. vacuum breaker
    C. pneumatic ejector
    D. comminutor

20. The flow of ground water into sanitary sewers through defective joints is called

    A. back siphonage
    B. infiltration
    C. overflow
    D. exfiltration

21. In a combined sewer system, the amount of sewage flowing to the treatment plant is USUALLY controlled by a

    A. regulator
    B. bar screen
    C. siphon
    D. mud valve

22. The LOWEST portion of the inside of a sewer pipe is the

    A. crown
    B. haunch
    C. invert
    D. spring line

23. A.C pipe, sometimes used instead of clay sewer pipe, is made of

    A. reinforced concrete
    B. polyvinyl
    C. asbestos and cement
    D. asphalt

24. Of the following, the one which is NOT a sewer cleaning tool is the

    A. gouge
    B. wire brush
    C. pilaster
    D. claw

25. A sewer rodding machine has speeds up to 100 FPM. As used here, FPM is an abbreviation for feet per

    A. million
    B. mile
    C. minute
    D. module

KEY (CORRECT ANSWERS)

1.	B	11.	C
2.	D	12.	A
3.	A	13.	D
4.	D	14.	C
5.	D	15.	C
6.	C	16.	C
7.	B	17.	C
8.	B	18.	B
9.	D	19.	C
10.	B	20.	B

21. A
22. C
23. C
24. C
25. C

TEST 2

DIRECTIONS: Each question or incomplete statement is followed by several suggested answers or completions. Select the one that BEST answers the question or completes the statement. *PRINT THE LETTER OF THE CORRECT ANSWER IN THE SPACE AT THE RIGHT.*

1. Wellpoints are used in sewer construction PRIMARILY to
    A. remove gases
    B. dewater trenches
    C. locate wells
    D. replace hydrants

2. A sewer which carries only sewage from the plumbing fixtures in a house is a
    A. storm sewer
    B. combined sewer
    C. sanitary sewer
    D. subsurface drain

3. The slope of a sewer is MOST usually indicated by the units,
    A. feet   B. rods   C. percent   D. diameters

4. Longitudinal timbers used to support the vertical sheeting in a sewer trench excavation are called
    A. wales
    B. cross braces
    C. piles
    D. cradles

5. The nominal diameter of a #4 reinforcing bar is MOST NEARLY
    A. 0.4"   B. 0.04"   C. 0.5"   D. 4 mm

6. In a 1:2:3 concrete mix, the number 3 represents the proportion of
    A. sand
    B. water
    C. coarse aggregate
    D. cement

7. When investigating a complaint by a homeowner of sewage backing up in a house, you find that the house trap in the basement is blocked.
   Of the following, the PROPER action for you to take is to
    A. call in a plumber for the homeowner
    B. clean out the house trap
    C. tell the homeowner to call in a plumber
    D. disconnect the house trap from the piping, clean it out, and reinstall the trap

8. Your men should be careful not to break manhole covers.
   Of the following, the BEST reason for taking this precaution is that
    A. the cost of the manhole cover will be taken out of your paycheck
    B. the manhole cover can't be replaced
    C. manhole covers cost money to replace
    D. broken manhole covers are difficult to get rid of

9. You are to report immediately by telephone if a manhole cover or basin grate is missing. Of the following, the BEST reason for having this requirement is to

   A. permit the cover or grate to be ordered if it is not on hand
   B. be able to assess the responsibility for this condition
   C. prevent an accident
   D. enable the Sanitation Department to clean the street

10. Of the following, the LEAST serious of the defects filed in a sewer report is

    A. broken casting
    B. missing casting
    C. noisy manhole cover
    D. backed up sewer

11. Of the following, the BEST method for a foreman to use to teach a man how to lift a manhole cover safely is to

    A. tell him how to do it
    B. make a sketch showing the correct method to use
    C. actually lift a cover with the man watching
    D. let the man try to lift the cover and correct any mistakes

12. Assume that you are training a group of men on the adjustment of a high-pressure relief valve.
    Of the following, the FIRST topic you should discuss with the men is

    A. the conditions under which it is necessary to adjust the relief valve
    B. how to order parts for the relief valve
    C. how the springs in the relief valve work
    D. how to take apart the relief valve

13. If four men work seven hours during the day, the number of man-hours of work done is

    A. 4   B. 7   C. 11   D. 28

14. If it takes four men fourteen days to do a certain job, seven men, working at the same rate, should be able to do the same job in _____ days.

    A. 8   B. 7   C. 6   D. 5

15. A truck leaves the garage at 9:26 A.M. and returns the same day at 3:43 P.M. The period of time that the truck was away from the garage is MOST NEARLY _____ hours _____ minutes.

    A. 5; 17   B. 5; 43   C. 6; 17   D. 6; 26

16. The sum of 2 5/8, 3 3/16, 1 1/2, and 4 1/4 is

    A. 9 13/16   B. 10 7/16   C. 11 9/16   D. 13 3/16

17. Of the following, a procedure used for causing air to flow into and from the lungs of the body by mechanical or manual methods is called

    A. irrigation
    B. traction
    C. traumatic shock
    D. artificial respiration

18. The one of the following that is a toxic gas which is colorless and odorless is   18._____

    A. chlorine
    B. hydrogen sulfide
    C. carbon monoxide
    D. gasoline

19. In first aid, a tourniquet is MOST often used to   19._____

    A. improve respiration
    B. treat burns
    C. treat sprains
    D. control bleeding

20. Persons who have been injured may suffer a depressed condition of many of the body functions due to failure of enough blood to circulate through the body. This condition is called   20._____

    A. immunization
    B. chronic
    C. cathartic
    D. shock

21. The type of injury which is MOST likely to cause lockjaw (tetanus) is   21._____

    A. an epileptic convulsion
    B. a puncture wound
    C. an electric shock
    D. sunstroke

22. If filling out an accident form, there is a section entitled *Accident Type*. Of the following, the one that is an accident type is   22._____

    A. struck by falling object
    B. operated without authority
    C. worked too slowly
    D. engaged in horseplay

23. On an accident report, there is an item labeled *Nature of Injury*. Of the following, the one that belongs in this category is   23._____

    A. fracture
    B. carelessness
    C. defective equipment
    D. loose clothing

24. Assume that the men you supervise are cleaning out a catch basin and uncover a gun. Of the following, the BEST action to take is to   24._____

    A. notify the Police Department of the discovery
    B. throw the gun away because it probably does not work
    C. keep the gun since you may be able to repair it
    D. dismantle the gun before disposing of it because it may be loaded

25. Assume that a new piece of mechanical equipment is brought to the job. Of the following, the BEST way for the men to learn the proper use of the equipment is to   25._____

    A. have a representative of the company that manufactures the equipment come to the job and demonstrate its use
    B. let the men try out the equipment and learn the operation of the equipment by using it
    C. let the men read the instruction manual carefully before trying out the equipment
    D. deliver a lecture to the men that have to use the equipment on the proper use of the equipment

KEY (CORRECT ANSWERS)

1. B
2. C
3. C
4. A
5. C

6. C
7. C
8. C
9. C
10. C

11. C
12. A
13. D
14. A
15. C

16. C
17. D
18. C
19. D
20. D

21. B
22. A
23. A
24. A
25. A

EXAMINATION SECTION
TEST 1

DIRECTIONS: Each question or incomplete statement is followed by several suggested answers or completions. Select the one that BEST answers the question or completes the statement. *PRINT THE LETTER OF THE CORRECT ANSWER IN THE SPACE AT THE RIGHT.*

1. When filling an empty aqueduct, the valve should be opened

    A. slowly to prevent damage to the aqueduct
    B. rapidly to fill the line as soon as possible
    C. slowly to prevent rapid lowering of the reservoir level
    D. rapidly so that there are no air locks

2. The BEST way of detecting the location of a suspected chlorine leak is by placing a _____ near the suspected leak.

    A. rag, which has been dipped in a strong ammonia water,
    B. match
    C. piece of litmus paper
    D. flow meter

3. The term *run-off* refers to the

    A. amount a valve must be turned in order to open it fully
    B. length of time an electric motor continues to turn after the current is shut off
    C. amount of rainfall which flows from the ground surface into the streams and reservoirs
    D. distance the water falls from the intake gate to the turbine

4. Algae in reservoirs may be killed by using

    A. zeolite
    B. copper sulphate
    C. sodium chloride
    D. calcium chloride

5. The one of the following types of valves that USUALLY operates without manual control is a(n) _____ valve.

    A. check   B. globe   C. gate   D. angle

6. Rate of flow of water through a water treatment plant is USUALLY referred to in terms of

    A. c.f.s.   B. c.f.m.   C. r.p.m.   D. m.g.d.

7. In order to make it easier to operate a large valve or gate, pressures on both sides of the valve or gate are balanced by

    A. using weights on each side of the valve or gate
    B. opening a smaller by-pass valve
    C. partially shutting down the water in the upstream line
    D. opening the downstream valve very slowly

8. Leaves are removed from the water entering the treatment plant or aqueduct by

    A. skimming   B. coagulating   C. draining   D. screening

9. Odors, due to gases in the water, are removed by 9.____

   A. surging B. sluicing C. aerating D. clarifying

10. Chlorine residual refers to the 10.____

   A. amount of chlorine that must be added to the water
   B. amount of chlorine that remains in the water after a given period
   C. method of adding the chlorine to the water
   D. method of protecting personnel using chlorine from the effects of the chlorine

11. One of the processes that takes place in an Imhoff tank is 11.____

   A. oxidation B. flocculation C. digestion D. coagulation

12. As used in a sewage disposal plant, *effluent* refers to the 12.____

   A. basic treatment process of sewage
   B. time it takes for complete treatment of sewage
   C. type of control the plant uses for treatment
   D. final liquid coming out of the treatment process

13. A grit chamber operates on the basis that 13.____

   A. grit will settle out of slow-moving water
   B. grit will float and can be removed by skimming the surface
   C. increasing the rate of flow of water will leave the grit behind
   D. spraying water into the air will cause the heavier grit to separate from the water

14. The purpose of sedimentation in any sewage treatment process is to 14.____

   A. aerate the sewage
   B. increase the chlorine content of the sewage
   C. remove suspended matter from the sewage
   D. kill the bacteria in the sewage

15. The final treatment for sludge before it is disposed of is 15.____

   A. drying B. adding chlorine
   C. mixing D. washing

16. The amount of sewage applied to a filter bed is GENERALLY controlled by a 16.____

   A. sluice gate B. flow meter
   C. dosing siphon D. regulating valve

17. Methane gas which results from the sewage treatment process is MOST frequently 17.____

   A. vented to the outside air to prevent injury to plant personnel
   B. used as a fuel in the plant
   C. combined with other gases to render it harmless
   D. burned in the open air

18. The filtering material in a *filter bed* at a sewage treat-ment plant is USUALLY 18.____

   A. activated charcoal B. sand
   C. alum D. ammonium chloride

19. Cleaning sewer lines is USUALLY done by the use of a

    A. catch basin
    B. flushometer
    C. sewer rod
    D. center line

20. One of the ways of locating a leak in a water line is by using a

    A. manometer
    B. sounding rod
    C. poling board
    D. diffusor

21. MOST sewer pipes are made of

    A. cast iron
    B. agricultural tile
    C. brass
    D. copper

22. One of the materials generally used in caulking joints in bell and spigot pipe is

    A. tar   B. litharge   C. red lead   D. oakum

23. Water pipe must be laid at least two feet below the ground surface MAINLY to

    A. prevent freezing
    B. discourage malicious tampering
    C. reduce the pressure required to make the water flow
    D. eliminate possibility of damage to roads in case of water main break

24. When soldering copper gutters, the flux that is GENERALLY used is

    A. sal ammoniac
    B. resin
    C. killed muriatic acid
    D. calcium chloride

25. A good concrete mix for use in the foundations of a small building is

    A. 1:2:5   B. 5:2:1   C. 2:5:1   D. 1:5:2

26. When painting steel, red lead is used MAINLY as a

    A. primer coat so final coat will adhere better
    B. primer coat to protect the steel from rusting
    C. finish coat to protect the steel from the action of the sun and water
    D. second coat to bind the primer and finish coats

27. Studs in frame buildings are USUALLY

    A. 1" x 4"   B. 1" x 6"   C. 2" x 4"   D. 2" x 6"

28. A cement mortar used in brickwork is USUALLY made more workable by adding

    A. phosphate   B. lime   C. calcium   D. grout

Questions 29-32.

DIRECTIONS: The following four questions numbered 29 to 32, inclusive, are to be answered in accordance with the rules of the department of water supply, gas and electricity.

29. The term *water course* refers to 29.____

   A. aqueducts only
   B. pipe lines only
   C. natural or artificial streams only
   D. all of the above

30. Where a swimming pool discharges upon or into the ground and the water is not treated, 30.____
    the minimum distance between such discharge and a stream MUST be at least _____
    feet.

   A. 50   B. 100   C. 250   D. 450

31. According to the above rules, clothes may 31.____

   A. be washed in a spring, if the spring does not feed directly into a reservoir
   B. be washed in a spring if the place where this is being done is at least one mile from a reservoir
   C. be washed in a spring provided a chlorinated soap is used
   D. not be washed in a spring

32. Industrial wastes may 32.____

   A. be discharged into a stream provided the stream does not feed directly into a reservoir
   B. be discharged into a stream, provided the point of discharge is at least one mile from a reservoir
   C. be discharged into a stream if the wastes are purified in an approved manner
   D. not be discharged into a stream

33. One method of determining the height of the water in a stream feeding into a reservoir is 33.____
    by means of a

   A. venturi meter   B. flow meter
   C. hook gage   D. strain gage

34. When digging a deep trench, the sides are USUALLY prevented from caving in by using 34.____

   A. shoulders   B. blocking   C. pins   D. sheathing

35. The FIRST precaution a worker should take before entering a sewer manhole is to 35.____

   A. put on hard-toed shoes
   B. put on safety goggles
   C. check that the next manhole upstream is not obstructed
   D. test the air in the manhole

36. Assume that a fuse blows upon connecting a light load to the circuit. You replace it with 36.____
    the same size fuse, and again the fuse blows.
    The BEST thing to do in this case is to

   A. connect a wire across the fuse so it cannot blow under such a light load
   B. replace the fuse with one having a higher rating
   C. check the wiring of the circuit
   D. place two fuses in series to prevent blowing

37. Of the following material, the one that is BEST for fill as a subgrade for a road is　　37.____

    A. sand
    B. silt
    C. clay
    D. a mixture of sand, silt, and clay

38. When dealing with leaking chlorine, it is IMPORTANT to remember that chlorine is　　38.____

    A. highly flammable
    B. made safe by spraying water on it
    C. not corrosive
    D. heavier than air

39. Cast iron pipe is MOST frequently cut with a(n)　　39.____

    A. hack saw
    B. diamond point chisel
    C. burning torch
    D. abrasive wheel

40. Water hammer in a pipe line is BEST reduced by installing　　40.____

    A. a pressure regulator
    B. an air chamber
    C. smaller pipes and valves
    D. larger pipes and valves

KEY (CORRECT ANSWERS)

1. A	11. C	21. A	31. D
2. A	12. D	22. D	32. D
3. C	13. A	23. A	33. C
4. B	14. C	24. C	34. D
5. A	15. A	25. A	35. D
6. D	16. C	26. B	36. C
7. B	17. B	27. C	37. D
8. D	18. B	28. B	38. D
9. C	19. C	29. D	39. B
10. B	20. B	30. B	40. B

TEST 2

DIRECTIONS: Each question or incomplete statement is followed by several suggested answers or completions. Select the one that BEST answers the question or completes the statement. *PRINT THE LETTER OF THE CORRECT ANSWER IN SPACE AT THE RIGHT.*

1. When used in conjunction with a centrifugal pump, a foot valve 1.____

   A. equalizes the pressure on both sides of the pump
   B. regulates the amount of water flowing through the pump
   C. prevents water in the pump from flowing back down the suction line
   D. adjusts the speed of the pump to the amount of water to be pumped

2. Grounding an electric motor is 2.____

   A. *good* practice because the motor will operate better
   B. *poor* practice because the motor will not operate as well
   C. *good* practice because it protects against shock hazards
   D. *poor* practice because it increases shock hazards

3. The one of the following wrenches that should NOT be used to turn a nut is a wrench. 3.____

   A. monkey   B. box   C. stillson   D. socket

4. A drill is GENERALLY removed from the chuck of a portable electric drill by using a 4.____

   A. drift pin   B. wedge
   C. centerpunch   D. key

5. The finished surface of a dirt road is MOST frequently maintained with a 5.____

   A. blade grader   B. bulldozer
   C. dragline   D. carryall

6. Frequent stalling of a truck engine is MOST probably due to a 6.____

   A. weak battery   B. low battery water level
   C. leaking oil filter   D. dirty carburetor

7. If the reading of the oil pressure gage on a gasoline motor should suddenly drop to zero, the FIRST thing the operator should do is to 7.____

   A. check the filter
   B. inspect the oil lines
   C. tighten the oil pan bolts
   D. stop the motor

8. A tractor is to be stored for two months. In order to keep it in BEST condition, it should be 8.____

   A. drained of all fuel and oil
   B. lubricated every week
   C. started up periodically and run until warm
   D. steam cleaned and all water drained from the radiator

9. Trees suffering from transplanting shock are quickly helped by 9.____

A. deep watering B. foliage feeding
C. root feeding D. vitamin treatments

10. For MOST rapid healing, trees should be pruned during

    A. November, December, and January
    B. February, March, and April
    C. May, June, and July
    D. August, September, and October

11. The blades of a lawn mower should be set so that the blades

    A. firmly touch the bed knife
    B. barely touch the bed knife
    C. clear the bed knife by 1/16 inch
    D. clear the bed knife by 1/8 inch

12. The MAIN reason for mulching is to

    A. fertilize the soil
    B. prevent erosion
    C. protect plants from the cold
    D. kill insects

13. A compost heap would MOST likely include

    A. lawn clippings B. sand
    C. stumps of trees D. gravel

14. Of the following statements with regard to *seeding,* the one that is CORRECT is:

    A. Seeds should be sown on a windy day
    B. The ground should be watered heavily after seeding
    C. Seeding should be done primarily on a bright and sunny day
    D. It is not necessary to carefully apportion the amount of seeds sown

15. Organic matter is often added to soil to better condition it for growing plants. Of the following, the item that is NOT organic matter is

    A. lime B. peat C. manure D. leaf mold

16. Of the following, the BEST way to store coniferous seedlings which cannot be planted for a few days is to

    A. unwrap them and put them in a dark, dry location
    B. place them flat on the ground in a sunny location so they can get plenty of light and air
    C. place them in a trench dug in the earth and cover the root ends with soil
    D. make sure the ball is not loosened and keep in a hothouse

17. Transplanting of seedlings is BEST done in early

    A. spring B. summer C. autumn D. winter

18. After planting privet hedges, they are frequently cut back to within a few inches of the ground.
    This is USUALLY done to

    A. remove dead parts of the hedge
    B. insure dense growth from the ground up
    C. speed up root development
    D. reduce the possibility of insect damage while the hedge is taking root

    18.____

19. *Heaving* of pavements in wintertime is USUALLY caused by the

    A. difference of expansion of pavement and subgrade
    B. freezing of water in subgrade
    C. loss of bond between pavement and subgrade
    D. brittleness of pavement

    19.____

20. Erosion of side slopes caused by the action of water is GREATEST when the soil is

    A. silt   B. clay   C. hardpan   D. silty-clay

    20.____

21. The MAIN reason for making a crown in a road pavement is to

    A. reduce the amount of paving material necessary
    B. make it easier for cars to go around a curve
    C. drain surface water
    D. increase the strength of the pavement where it is most needed

    21.____

22. The MAIN reason for paving ditches at the side of a road is to

    A. prevent damage from cars
    B. permit the ditch to carry more water
    C. prevent erosion of the soil in the ditch
    D. block water from getting under the pavement

    22.____

23. Assume that vitrified clay tile pipe, with open joints, is being used as the underdrain for a roadway.
    This pipe should be laid

    A. directly on the bottom of the trench
    B. on a bed of clay
    C. on a bed of peat
    D. on a bed of gravel

    23.____

24. A macadam road is one in which the base is GENERALLY made of

    A. asphalt   B. broken stone
    C. concrete   D. stabilized soil

    24.____

25. To loosen compacted rocky earth road surfaces, the BEST piece of equipment to use is a

    A. disc harrow   B. drag line   C. bulldozer   D. scarifier

    25.____

26. Oiling of an earth road is BEST done

    A. in the winter before the snow falls
    B. when you expect much rain

    26.____

C. in the spring during dry weather
D. immediately after snow is cleared from the road

27. Cracks in concrete roads are BEST repaired by filling them with

    A. tar
    B. grout
    C. mineral filler
    D. sand

28. When repairing patches in old asphalt pavements, the edges of the patch should FIRST be painted with

    A. the same material used for the patch
    B. kerosene
    C. asphalt cement
    D. asphalt binder

29. The sum of 3 1/4, 5 1/8, 2 1/2, and 3 3/8 is

    A. 14   B. 14 1/8   C. 14 1/4   D. 14 3/8

30. Assume that it takes 6 men 8 days to do a particular job.
    If you have only 4 men available to do this job and they all work at the same speed, then the number of days it would take to complete the job would be

    A. 11   B. 12   C. 13   D. 14

31. The city aims to supply *potable* water. As used in this sentence, the word *potable* means MOST NEARLY

    A. clear   B. drinkable   C. fresh   D. adequate

32. Water, after being purified, should not be turbid. As used in this sentence, the word turbid means MOST NEARLY

    A. cloudy   B. warm   C. infected   D. hard

33. The flow of water is *impeded* by the silt in the bottom of the stream.
    As used in this sentence, the word *impeded* means MOST NEARLY

    A. dammed   B. hindered   C. helped   D. dirtied

Questions 34-35.

DIRECTIONS: Questions 34 and 35 are based on the following paragraph.

Repeated burning of the same area should be avoided. Burning should not be done on impervious, shallow, unstable, or highly erodible soils, or on steep slopes - especially in areas subject to heavy rains or rapid snowmelt. When existing vegetation is likely to be killed or seriously weakened by the fire, measures should be taken to assure prompt revegetation of the burned area. Burns should be limited to relatively small proportions of a watershed unit so that the stream channels will be able to carry any increased flows with a minimum of damage.

34. According to the above paragraph, planned burning should be limited to small areas of the watershed because

    A. the fire can be better controlled
    B. existing vegetation will be less likely to be killed
    C. plants will grow quicker in small areas
    D. there will be less likelihood of damaging floods

35. According to the above paragraph, burning usually should be done on soils that

    A. readily absorb moisture
    B. have been burnt before
    C. exist as a thin layer over rock
    D. can be flooded by nearby streams

36. If a foreman does not understand the instructions that are given to him by the district engineer, the BEST thing to do is to

    A. work out the solution to the problem himself
    B. do the job in the way he thinks is best
    C. get one of the other foremen to do the job
    D. ask that the instructions be repeated and clarified

37. The BEST foreman is the one who

    A. can work as fast as the fastest man in the crew
    B. is the most skilled mechanic
    C. can get the most work out of the men
    D. is the strongest man

38. Complimenting a man for good work is

    A. *good* practice since it will give the man an incentive to continue working well
    B. *poor* practice because the other men will become jealous
    C. *good* practice because in the future the foreman will not have to supervise this man
    D. *poor* practice since the man should work well without needing compliments

39. In dealing with his men, it is MOST important that a foreman be

    A. a disciplinarian   B. stern
    C. fair   D. chummy with his men

40. When issuing a violation to a member of the public, it is MOST important that a foreman be

    A. aloof and refuse to discuss the violation
    B. stern, and warn the person to correct the violation immediately
    C. courteous and explain what must be done to correct the violation
    D. friendly and volunteer assistance to correct the violation

KEY (CORRECT ANSWERS)

1. C	11. B	21. C	31. B
2. C	12. C	22. C	32. A
3. C	13. A	23. D	33. B
4. D	14. B	24. B	34. D
5. A	15. A	25. D	35. A
6. D	16. C	26. C	36. D
7. D	17. A	27. A	37. C
8. C	18. B	28. C	38. A
9. B	19. B	29. C	39. C
10. B	20. A	30. B	40. C

EXAMINATION SECTION
TEST 1

DIRECTIONS: Each question or incomplete statement is followed by several suggested answers or completions. Select the one that BEST answers the question or completes the statement. *PRINT THE LETTER OF THE CORRECT ANSWER IN THE SPACE AT THE RIGHT.*

1. The composition of plumber's solder for wiping is APPROXIMATELY (ratio of tin to lead) 1.____

   A. 40-60 B. 50-50 C. 60-40 D. 70-30

2. A device used to lift sewage to the level of a sewer from a floor below the sewer grade is known as a(n) 2.____

   A. elevator B. ejector C. sump D. conveyer

3. A check valve in a piping system will 3.____

   A. permit excessive pressures in a boiler
   B. eliminate water hammer
   C. permit water to flow in only one direction
   D. control the rate of flow of water

4. The chemical MOST frequently used to clean drains clogged with grease is 4.____

   A. muriatic acid B. soda ash
   C. ammonia D. caustic soda

5. To test for leaks in a newly installed C.I. waste stack, 5.____

   A. oil of peppermint is poured into the top of the stack
   B. smoke under pressure is pumped into the stack
   C. a water meter is used to measure the water flow
   D. dye is placed in the system at the top of the stack

6. When installing a catch basin, the outlet should be located 6.____

   A. at the same level as the inlet
   B. above the inlet
   C. below the inlet
   D. at the invert

7. The copper float in a low down water tank is perforated so that water enters the ball. As a result, the tank will 7.____

   A. flush once, and then will not operate again
   B. not flush at all
   C. not flush completely
   D. continue to flush, but water will be wasted

8. If water leaks from the stem of a faucet when the faucet is opened, the _____ should be 8.____

   A. faucet; replaced B. cap nut; rethreaded
   C. seat; reground D. packing; replaced

9. In a hot water heating system, it may be necessary to *bleed* radiators to

   A. relieve high steam pressure
   B. permit entrapped, air to escape
   C. allow condensate to return to the boiler
   D. drain off waste water

10. When painting raw wood, puttying of nail holes should be done

    A. 24 hours before the prime coat
    B. immediately before the prime coat
    C. after the prime coat and before the second coat
    D. after the second coat and before the finish

11. In general, the one of the following that will dry *tack free* in the SHORTEST time is

    A. lacquer   B. varnish   C. enamel   D. oil paint

12. The *vehicle* MOST frequently used in paints for exterior wood surfaces is

    A. white lead   B. linseed oil
    C. japan   D. varnish

13. Painting of an interior plastered wall is usually delayed until the plaster is dry. If this practice is NOT followed, the paint might

    A. chalk   B. fade   C. run   D. blister

14. A *sealer* applied over knots and pitch streaks to prevent *bleeding* through paint is

    A. shellac   B. lacquer
    C. coal tar   D. carnauba wax

15. Painting of outside steel in near freezing (32° F) weather is poor practice MAINLY because

    A. the paint will not dry properly
    B. ice will form in the thinner
    C. more paint is required
    D. paint fumes are dangerous

16. When repainting exterior woodwork that has a glossy finish, good adhesion of paint is BEST obtained by first

    A. *washing* the work with diluted lye
    B. *dulling* the work with sandpaper
    C. *warming* the work with an electric heater
    D. *roughening* the work with a rasp

17. The one of the following methods of cleaning steelwork prior to painting that is NOT commonly used on exterior work, such as bridges, is

    A. sandblasting   B. flame cleaning
    C. wire brushing   D. pickling

18. When spraying oil paints, the type of gun and nozzle preferred is a _____ feed gun, _____ mix nozzle.

    A. pressure; internal
    B. pressure, external
    C. syphon; internal
    D. syphon; external

19. When opening a bag of cement, you find that the cement is lumpy.
    The cement should be

    A. discarded and not used at all
    B. crushed before placing in the mixer
    C. used as is since the mixer will grind it
    D. well mixed with water and stored overnight before using

20. A 1:2:4 concrete mix by volume is specified.
    If 6 cubic feet of cement is to be used in the mix, the volume of sand to use is, in cubic feet,

    A. 3 B. 6 C. 12 D. 24

21. Honeycombing in concrete is BEST prevented by

    A. increasing water-cement ratio
    B. heating concrete in cold weather
    C. using mechanical vibrators
    D. adding calcium chloride

22. When a lightweight concrete is required, the one of the following that is COMMONLY used as an aggregate is

    A. gravel B. brick chips C. stone D. cinders

23. A rubbed finish on concrete is USUALLY obtained by use of a

    A. carborundum brick
    B. garnet sanding belt
    C. fibre brush and wax
    D. pad of steel wool

24. A copper strip is frequently embedded in the concrete across a construction joint in a concrete wall.
    The purpose of this is to

    A. make a watertight joint
    B. bond the two parts of the wall together
    C. prevent unequal settlement
    D. retard temperature cracking

25. In brickwork laid in common bond, a header course USUALLY occurs in every _____ course.

    A. 2nd B. 4th C. 6th D. 8th

26. Pointing of brickwork refers to

    A. cutting brick to fit
    B. patching mortar joints
    C. attaching brick veneer
    D. arranging brick in an arch

27. Furring is applied to brick walls to

    A. strengthen the wall
    B. waterproof the wall
    C. provide ventilation to prevent condensation
    D. provide a base for lathing

28. The FIRST coat in plaster work is *scratched* in order to

    A. remove excess plaster
    B. smooth the base for the second coat
    C. provide a bond for the second coat
    D. strengthen the base coat

29. An alloy used where resistance to corrosion is important is

    A. tungsten   B. mild steel   C. monel   D. tin

30. The size of iron pipe is given in terms of its nominal

    A. weight   B. inside diameter
    C. outside diameter D. wall thickness

31. When preparing surfaces to be soldered, the FIRST step is

    A. tinning   B. sweating   C. heating   D. cleaning

32. To test for leaks in an acetylene torch, it is BEST that one use

    A. soapy water   B. a match
    C. a gas with a strong odor D. a pressure gauge

33. One advantage of using a Pittsburgh lock seam when joining two pieces of sheet metal is that, once formed in the shop, it may be assembled anywhere with a

    A. hickey   B. swage   C. template   D. mallet

34. White cast iron is

    A. hard and brittle   B. hard and ductile
    C. ductile and malleable D. brittle and malleable

35. The gage used for measuring copper wire is

    A. U.S. Standard   B. Stubbs
    C. Washburn and Moen   D. Brown and Sharpe

36. The BEST flux to use when soldering copper wires in an electric circuit is

    A. sal ammoniac   B. zinc chloride
    C. rosin   D. borax

37. The spark test, to determine the approximate composition of an unknown metal, is made by

    A. holding the metal against a grinding wheel
    B. striking flint on the unknown metal
    C. connecting wires from a source of electric power to the metal and striking an arc with a bare wire
    D. heating with an oxyacetylene torch

38. The one of the following metals that is MOST commonly used for bearings is

    A. duraluminum B. brass C. babbit D. lead

39. A *tailstock* is found on a

    A. drill press B. shaper C. planer D. lathe

40. The BEST lubricant to use when cutting screw threads in steel is

    A. naphtha
    C. lard oil
    B. 3-in-1 oil
    D. linseed oil

41. When a high speed cutting tool is required, the tip is frequently made of

    A. carborundum
    C. bronze
    B. tungsten carbide
    D. vanadium

42. A nut is turned on a 3/4"-10 bolt.
    When the nut is turned five complete turns on this bolt, the distance it moves along the bolt

    A. depends on the type of thread
    C. is 0.375 inches
    B. is 0.2 inches
    D. is 0.5 inches

43. Of the following, the STRONGEST screw thread form is the

    A. Whitworth
    C. National Standard
    B. Acme
    D. V

44. *Knurling* refers to

    A. rolling depressions in a fixed pattern on a cylindrical surface
    B. turning between centers on a lathe
    C. making deep cuts in a flat plate with a milling machine
    D. drilling matching holes in bolt and nut for a cotter pin

45. A special device used to guide the drill as well as to hold the work when drilling is known as a

    A. dolly B. jig C. chuck D. collet

46. Tools that have a *Morse taper* would be used on a

    A. milling machine
    C. planer
    B. shaper
    D. drill press

47. When tapping a blind hole in a plate, the FIRST tap to use is a

    A. plug B. bottoming C. lead D. taper

48. An important safety practice to remember when cutting a rivet with a chisel is to wear

    A. leather gloves
    C. cup goggles
    B. steel toe shoes
    D. a hard hat

49. Electricians working around *live wires* should wear gloves made of 49.____
    A. asbestos   B. metal mesh   C. leather   D. rubber

50. Storage of oily rags presents a safety hazard because of possible 50.____
    A. fire
    C. attraction of rats
    B. poisonous flames
    D. leakage of oil

KEY (CORRECT ANSWERS)

1. A	11. A	21. C	31. D	41. B
2. B	12. B	22. D	32. A	42. D
3. C	13. D	23. A	33. D	43. B
4. D	14. A	24. A	34. A	44. A
5. B	15. A	25. C	35. B	45. B
6. C	16. B	26. B	36. C	46. D
7. D	17. D	27. D	37. A	47. D
8. D	18. A	28. C	38. C	48. C
9. B	19. A	29. C	39. D	49. D
10. C	20. C	30. B	40. C	50. A

TEST 2

DIRECTIONS: Each question or incomplete statement is followed by several suggested answers or completions. Select the one that BEST answers the question or completes the statement. *PRINT THE LETTER OF THE CORRECT ANSWER IN THE SPACE AT THE RIGHT.*

1. *Shimmying* of the front wheels of a truck is MOST frequently caused by 1.____

    A. worn front brake drums
    B. a worn differential gear
    C. a loose steering gear
    D. a dead shock absorber

2. The MOST important reason for maintaining correct air pressure in all tires of a truck is to 2.____

    A. prevent the truck from swerving when brakes are applied
    B. permit the truck to stop quicker in an emergency
    C. provide a smoother ride
    D. prevent excessive wear on the tires

3. The oil gage on the dashboard of a truck indicates 3.____

    A. the amount of oil in the pan
    B. the pressure at which the oil is being pumped
    C. if the oil filter is working
    D. the temperature of the oil in the motor

4. An unbalanced wheel on a truck is corrected by 4.____

    A. bending the rim slightly
    B. adjusting the king pin
    C. changing the ratio of caster to camber
    D. adding small weights to the rim

5. A cold motor on a truck should be warmed up in wintertime by 5.____

    A. turning on the heater and pouring warm water into the radiator
    B. allowing the motor to idle for a few minutes
    C. racing the motor
    D. alternately pressing the gas pedal to the floor and releasing it

6. The brake pedal on a truck goes to the floorboard when pushed. The one of the following that would cause this condition is 6.____

    A. air in the hydraulic system
    B. wet brakes
    C. excessive fluid in the cylinders
    D. a loose backing plate

7. The ammeter of a truck indicates no charge during operation even though the battery is run down. To find the fault, the generator field terminal is grounded. The ammeter now shows a charge. The part that is defective is the 7.____

    A. generator field coil
    B. armature
    C. brushes
    D. voltage regulator

8. The part used to control the ratio of air and gasoline in a truck engine is the

   A. bogie B. filter C. carburetor D. pump

9. The MAIN purpose of a vacuum booster on a truck engine is to

   A. increase the manifold vacuum
   B. assist windshield wiper operation
   C. provide a steadier fuel flow
   D. govern engine speed

10. The purpose of grounding the frame of an electric motor is to

    A. prevent excessive vibration
    B. eliminate shock hazards
    C. reduce power requirements
    D. prevent overheating

11. The one of the following that is NOT part of an electric motor is a

    A. brush B. rheostat C. pole D. commutator

12. An electrical transformer would be used to

    A. change current from AC to DC
    B. raise or lower the power
    C. raise or lower the voltage
    D. change the frequency

13. The piece of equipment that would be rated in ampere hours is a

    A. storage battery
    B. bus bar
    C. rectifier
    D. capacitor

14. A ballast is a necessity in a(n)

    A. motor generator set
    B. fluorescent lighting system
    C. oil circuit breaker
    D. synchronous converter

15. The power factor in an AC circuit is on when

    A. no current is flowing
    B. the voltage at the source is a minimum
    C. the voltage and current are in phase
    D. there is no load

16.

Neglecting the internal resistance in the battery, the current flowing through the battery shown in the sketch above is _____ amp.

   A. 3 B. 6 C. 9 D. 12

17. When excess current flows, a circuit breaker is opened directly by the action of a   17.____

    A. condenser   B. transistor   C. relay   D. solenoid

18. The MAIN purpose of bridging in building floor construction is to   18.____

    A. spread floor loads evenly to joists
    B. reduce the number of joists required
    C. permit use of thinner subflooring
    D. reduce noise passage through floors

19. Of the following, the material MOST commonly used for subflooring is   19.____

    A. rock lath   B. insulation board
    C. plywood   D. transite

20. In connection with stair construction, the one of the following that is LEAST related to the others is   20.____

    A. tread   B. cap   C. nosing   D. riser

21. The type of nail MOST commonly used in flooring is   21.____

    A. common   B. cut   C. brad   D. casing

22. The edge joint of flooring boards is COMMONLY   22.____

    A. mortise and tenon   B. shiplap
    C. half lap   D. tongue and groove

23. The purpose of a ridge board in building construction is to   23.____

    A. locate corners of a building
    B. keep plaster work smooth
    C. support the ends of roof rafters
    D. conceal openings at the eaves

24. To prevent splintering of wood when using an auger bit,   24.____

    A. the bit should be hollow ground
    B. hold the piece of wood in a vise
    C. clamp a piece of scrap wood to the back of the piece being drilled
    D. use a slow speed on the drill press

25. End grain of a post can be MOST easily planed by use of a _____ plane.   25.____

    A. rafter   B. jack   C. fore   D. block

26. A butt gauge is used when   26.____

    A. hanging doors   B. laying out stairs
    C. making rafter cuts   D. framing studs

27. The one of the following grades of sandpaper with the FINEST grit is   27.____

    A. 0   B. 2/0   C. 1/2   D. 1

28. The sum of the following numbers, 3 7/8, 14 1/4, 6 7/16, 22 3/16, 8 1/2 is   28.____

    A. 55 1/16   B. 55 1/8   C. 55 3/16   D. 55 1/4

29. The area of the rectangular field shown in the diagram at the right is, in square feet,   29.____

    437 FT.

    68 ft

    A. 29,456
    B. 29,626
    C. 29,716
    D. 29,836

30. The cost of material is approximately 3/8ths of the total cost of a certain job. If the total cost of the job is $127.56, then the cost of material is MOST NEARLY   30.____

    A. $47.83   B. $48.24   C. $48.65   D. $49.06

31. A blueprint is drawn to a scale of 1/4" = 1'0". A line on the blueprint that is not dimensioned is measured with a ruler and found to be 3 3/8" long.   31.____
    The length represented by this line is

    A. 13'2"   B. 13'4"   C. 13'6"   D. 13'8"

32. A maintainer, in repairing a brick wall, spends one-half hour getting materials, forty-three minutes chipping and cleaning the wall, fifteen minutes mixing the mortar, and one hour and twenty-seven minutes in applying the brick and finishing.   32.____
    The total time spent on this repair job is _____ hours _____ minute(s).

    A. 2; 45   B. 2; 50   C. 2; 55   D. 3; 0

33. *Employees are responsible for the good care, proper maintenance, and <u>serviceable condition</u> of property issued or assigned to their use.*   33.____
    As used above, *serviceable condition* means MOST NEARLY

    A. capable of being repaired   B. fit for use
    C. ease of handling   D. minimum cost

34. *An employee shall be on the alert constantly for potential accident hazards.*   34.____
    As used above, *potential* means MOST NEARLY

    A. dangerous   B. careless   C. possible   D. frequent

Questions 35-37.

DIRECTIONS: Questions 35 to 37, inclusive, are to be answered in accordance with the following paragraph.

All cement work contracts, more or less, in setting. The contraction in concrete walls and other structures causes fine cracks to develop at regular intervals. The tendency to contract increases in direct proportion to the quantity of cement in the concrete. A rich mixture will contract more than a lean mixture. A concrete wall, which has been made of a very lean mixture and which has been built by filling only about one foot in depth of concrete in the form each day will frequently require close inspection to reveal the cracks.

35. According to the above paragraph,

    A. shrinkage seldom occurs in concrete
    B. shrinkage occurs only in certain types of concrete
    C. by placing concrete at regular intervals, shrinkage may be avoided
    D. it is impossible to prevent shrinkage

36. According to the above paragraph, the one of the factors which reduces shrinkage in concrete is the

    A. volume of concrete in wall
    B. height of each day's pour
    C. length of wall
    D. length and height of wall

37. According to the above paragraph, a rich mixture

    A. pours the easiest
    B. shows the largest amount of cracks
    C. is low in cement content
    D. need not be inspected since cracks are few

Questions 38-39.

DIRECTIONS: Questions 38 and 39 are to be answered in accordance with the following paragraph.

Painting is done to preserve surfaces, and unless the surface is properly prepared, good preservation will not be possible. Apply paint only to clean dry surfaces. After a surface has been scaled, which means that all loose paint and rust are removed by chipping, scraping, and wire brushing, be sure all dust and dirt are completely removed.

38. According to the above paragraph, the MAIN purpose of painting a wall is to _____ the wall.

    A. clean   B. waterproof
    C. protect   D. remove dust from

39. According to the above paragraph,

    A. chipping, scraping, and wire brushing are the only methods permitted for cleaning surfaces
    B. painting is effective only when the surface is clean
    C. scaling refers only to the removal of rust
    D. paint may be applied on wet surfaces

40. The order in which the dimensions of stock are listed on a bill of materials is

    A. thickness, length, and width   B. thickness, width, and length
    C. width, length, and thickness   D. length, thickness, and width

41. The glue that will BEST withstand extreme exposure to moisture and water is _____ glue.

    A. polyvinyl
    B. resorcinol
    C. powdered resin
    D. protein

42. Four board feet of lumber, listed at $350.00 per M, will cost

    A. $3.50   B. $1.40   C. $1.30   D. $4.00

43. The cap iron or chip breaker stiffens the plane iron and

    A. protects the cutting edge
    B. curls the shaving
    C. regulates the thickness of the shaving
    D. reduces mouth gap

44. Coping-saw blades have teeth shaped like those on a _____ saw.

    A. dovetail   B. crosscut   C. back   D. rip

45. Of the following, the claw hammer that is BEST suited for general use in a woodworking shop is the _____ claw.

    A. straight
    B. bell-faced curved
    C. plain-faced curved
    D. adze eye curved

46. The natural binder which cements wood fibers together and makes wood solid is

    A. cellulose
    B. lignin
    C. alpha-cellulose
    D. trichocarpa

47. The plane that is BEST suited for trimming the bottom of a dado or lap joint is the _____ plane.

    A. block   B. router   C. rabbet   D. core-box

48. Brads are fasteners that are similar to _____ nails.

    A. escutcheon
    B. box
    C. finishing
    D. duplex head

49. The plane in which the plane iron is inserted with its bevel in the up position is the _____ plane.

    A. fore   B. rabbet   C. block   D. circular

50. Coating materials used to protect wood against fire USUALLY contain a water soluble fire-retardant such as

    A. ammonium chloride
    B. sodium perborate
    C. sodium silicate
    D. sal soda

KEY (CORRECT ANSWERS)

1. C	11. B	21. B	31. C	41. B
2. D	12. C	22. D	32. C	42. B
3. B	13. A	23. C	33. B	43. B
4. D	14. B	24. C	34. C	44. D
5. B	15. C	25. D	35. D	45. B
6. A	16. A	26. A	36. B	46. B
7. D	17. D	27. B	37. B	47. B
8. C	18. A	28. D	38. C	48. C
9. B	19. C	29. C	39. B	49. C
10. B	20. B	30. A	40. B	50. C

EXAMINATION SECTION
TEST 1

DIRECTIONS: Each question or incomplete statement is followed by several suggested answers or completions. Select the one that BEST answers the question or completes the statement. *PRINT THE LETTER OF THE CORRECT ANSWER IN THE SPACE AT THE RIGHT.*

1. When making a preliminary inspection of a new street marking job, the FIRST thing to check is whether 1.____

   A. the location is correct
   B. all dimensions are correct
   C. the right paint is specified
   D. traffic can easily be controlled

2. After a preliminary inspection of a new street marking job has been made and it has been found that it can be laid out exactly as shown in the drawings received from Plans and Surveys, the site should be reinspected on the first day of actual work to check that 2.____

   A. the dimensions are correct according to the plans
   B. the orientation has not changed
   C. excavation work that did not exist on his first inspection does not obstruct his work
   D. the traffic can easily be controlled

3. Of the following, it is MOST important when inspecting the installation of a sign in a garage or on a street to check for the _____ the sign. 3.____

   A. correct width of
   B. correct area of
   C. correct mounting height of
   D. removal of all scuff marks below

4. When inspecting a job site in an off-street parking garage prior to starting a new job involving markings, the FIRST thing to look for is 4.____

   A. obstructions such as beams which will require that the layout be altered
   B. oil on the floor
   C. paint splashes on the floor
   D. vehicles which must be moved

5. The one of the following items which should be checked on a job involving the installation of custom-made highway guide signs but which need NOT be checked during the installation of street regulatory signs is the _____ of the sign. 5.____

   A. color
   B. wording and spelling
   C. width
   D. area

6. Assume that you are facing east while standing on the northwest corner of the intersection of two streets. One of these streets runs north and south, and the other runs east and west.
The SOUTHWEST corner of this intersection is 6.____

A. *directly* across the street in front of you
B. *directly* across the street to your right
C. *diagonally* across the intersection from you
D. *directly* across the street to your left

7. A street running north and south intersects a street running east and west. Four men designated as A, B, C, and D are each on a different corner of the intersection. A is on the NW corner and faces east; B is on the SW corner and faces north; C is on the SE corner and faces west; and D is on the NE corner and faces west.
The two men who are facing DIRECTLY toward each other are

A. A and B   B. B and C   C. C and D   D. A and D

8. Of the following, the MOST important item to check during a routine inspection of an air compressor is the

A. amount of air used daily
B. number of hours it has been operated
C. diaphragm diameter
D. condition of the paint finish

9. Assume that a crew assigned to you goes out to paint some street markings on a street which has a great deal of traffic.
The traffic should be diverted away from the working area by means of

A. Class I barricades
B. Class II barricades
C. Class I barricades and cones
D. cones

10. Assume that an extensive area within an off-street parking facility has caved in. Until repairs are completed, cars should be kept away from this area by means of

A. Class I barricades
B. Class I barricades and flasher lights
C. Class II barricades and cones
D. warning signs and Class I barricades

11. A line of traffic cones, being used to divert traffic fron men painting cross-walks in the lane nearest the curb, should begin at the curb at a point whose distance fron the working area is _____ feet, and the cones should be _____ feet apart.

A. 40; 10   B. 60; 15   C. 80; 15   D. 100; 10

12. Crews doing street marking work at night should wear

A. gray coveralls and set out traffic cones to divert traffic away from the area
B. reflectorized vests and set out traffic cones to divert traffic away from the area
C. bright yellow helmets and gray coveralls
D. bright blue helmets and set out traffic cones to divert traffic away from the area

13. Assume that the top of a 12 foot ladder is to be placed against a wall. The RECOMMENDED safe practice is that the ladder should be placed so that the distance from the bottom of the ladder to the base of the wall is _____ ft.

    A. 1   B. 2   C. 3   D. 5

14. According to the State Vehicle and Traffic Law, when driving at a speed of 40 miles per hour along a dry road, the driver should maintain a distance between his car and the car immediately ahead of him of AT LEAST _____ car lengths.

    A. 2   B. 3   C. 4   D. 5

15. Assume that a man has been knocked unconscious.
    Which of the following should NOT be done to the victim?

    A. Give him something to drink
    B. Hold a handkerchief with spirits of ammonia under his nose if he is breathing
    C. Keep him covered with a blanket
    D. Give him artificial respiration if he is not breathing

16. A paint sprayer may have gauges showing the pressure of the tank, the paint pressure, and the atomizer pressure. When the sprayer is operating properly, the

    A. paint pressure is higher than the tank pressure
    B. atomizer pressure is higher than the tank pressure
    C. paint and atomizer pressures are equal
    D. atomizer pressure is higher than the paint pressure

17. A certain paint can cover 310 square feet per gallon. The number of gallons of this paint required to paint 200 lines each 6 inches wide and 18 feet-6 inches long is MOST NEARLY

    A. 2   B. 4   C. 6   D. 8

18. Paint brushes that are used with an oil-based paint are USUALLY cleaned with

    A. turpentine   B. linseed oil
    C. acetone   D. alcohol

19. The air in an air compressor cylinder is DIRECTLY compressed by the

    A. pressure switch   B. surge chamber
    C. cam   D. piston

20. The part which permits the motor of an air compressor to start free of load regardless of the tank pressure is the

    A. unloader valve   B. surge tank
    C. pressure switch   D. drain cock

21. Assume that instead of spraying paint properly, a paint sprayer ejects a solid stream of paint from its nozzle. The one of the following that may cause this condition is

    A. compressor tank pressure is too high
    B. compressor tank pressure is lower than the atomizer pressure
    C. atomizer pressure is higher than the paint pressure
    D. atomizer pressure is too low

22. The one of the following which is a *regulatory* sign is the

    A. bump sign B. low clearance sign
    C. route marker D. stop sign

23. The one of the following which is a *regulatory* sign is the _____ sign.

    A. yield B. stop ahead
    C. side road D. slippery when wet

24. The one of the following signs which is octagonal is the _____ sign.

    A. speed limit B. stop ahead
    C. road narrows D. stop

25. Of the following statements, the one which gives the function of a *warning* sign is that this sign

    A. indicates route designations, destinations, or distances
    B. gives the driver notice of laws or regulations that apply at a given place, disregard of which is punishable as a violation or a misdemeanor
    C. calls attention to conditions in or adjacent to a street that are potentially hazardous to traffic
    D. indicates points of interest or geographical locations

26. The regulation manual on temporary traffic control of the department of traffic defines Class II barricades as being of the *horse* type with only one rail.
    It further specifies that the rail should be marked on

    A. *one* side with 3" vertical red and white, black and white, or black and yellow reflectorized stripes
    B. *both* sides with 3" vertical red and white, black and white, or black and yellow stripes
    C. *both* sides with 6" reflectorized red and white, black and white, or black and yellow stripes sloping at an angle of 45
    D. *both* sides with 6" vertical red and white or black and white stripes

27. Silk screening is a method of

    A. temporarily concealing signs already erected but not ready to be used
    B. painting signs
    C. protecting newly painted crosswalks until they dry
    D. protecting reflectorized signs from dust

28. The blade of a snow plow is USUALLY made of

    A. monel B. steel
    C. tungsten carbide D. beryllium

29. To PROPERLY check the lifting device of a snow plow at the beginning of the snow season, the plow blade should be

    A. raised and kept in that position for at least three minutes in order to detect leaks in the system
    B. raised by the lifting device once to see if it operates

C. dropped quickly after being brought to the raised position
D. raised and lowered and then the operation should be repeated

30. At the present time, the department of traffic USUALLY reflectorizes signs by   30._____

    A. coating the portion of the sign to be reflectorized with very tiny glass beads held by an adhesive base
    B. outlining the reflectorized portion of the sign with large glass *bull's eyes*
    C. making the reflectorized portion of the sign with *Scotch Lite*
    D. painting the reflectorized portion of the sign with *Luminar*

KEY (CORRECT ANSWERS)

1. A	11. D	21. D
2. C	12. B	22. D
3. C	13. C	23. A
4. A	14. C	24. D
5. B	15. A	25. C
6. B	16. D	26. C
7. D	17. C	27. B
8. B	18. A	28. B
9. D	19. D	29. A
10. C	20. A	30. C

TEST 2

DIRECTIONS: Each question or incomplete statement is followed by several suggested answers or completions. Select the one that BEST answers the question or completes the statement. *PRINT THE LETTER OF THE CORRECT ANSWER IN THE SPACE AT THE RIGHT.*

1. The material which causes the hydraulic plunger of a heavy duty hydraulic jack to move is
   A. oil
   b. petrolatum
   C. alcohol
   D. glycerol

   1.____

2. "Vapor Lock" will DIRECTLY affect the operation of
   A. air compressors
   B. pneumatic hammers
   C. paint sprayers
   D. automobiles

   2.____

3. Of the following grades of SAE crankcase oils, the one which is RECOMMENDED for year-round use is
   A. 10W-30
   B. 30
   C. 20W
   D. 10W

   3.____

4. Of the following, wheel misalignment in an automobile USUALLY results in
   A. frequent stalling
   B. improper clutch action
   C. rapid tire wear
   D. impaired shock absorber action

   4.____

5. Of the following, the EASIEST method of locating a defective spark plug in a gasoline engine is to
   A. take out all the spark plugs and examine them
   B. short circuit the spark plugs one at a time
   C. replace all of the spark plugs with new ones
   D. rotate all the spark plugs

   5.____

6. The one of the following conditions which may cause the fuel mixture in a gasoline engine to be too rich is
   A. water in the gasoline
   B. a dirty air cleaner
   C. a punctured muffler
   D. vapor lock in the fuel line

   6.____

7. If the battery of a car is constantly running dry, the one of the following items which should be checked FIRST is the
   A. generator
   B. ignition switch
   C. relay
   D. voltage regulator

   7.____

8. In a gasoline engine, the throttle vale is a part of the
   A. fuel tank
   B. carbureto
   C. crankcase
   D. water radiator

   8.____

9. If a car does not start on damp days, the trouble is MOST likely in the _____ system.
   A. ignition B. fuel C. lubricating D. cooling

10. The one of the following terms that applies to the relationship between the front axle and the steering mechanism of an automobile is
    A. camber B. armature C. crankshaft D. camshaft

11. The function of a carburetor on a gasoline engine is to
    A. filter the gasoline
    B. mix air and gasoline in the correct proportions
    C. pump the gasoline into the cylinder
    D. filter the air coming into the engine

12. An automotive ignition coil is used in the electrical system of a gasoline engine to
    A. reduce arcing across the breaker points
    B. transformers low voltage to high voltage
    C. operate the ignition switch
    D. charge the battery

13. The purpose of the thermostat in the cooling system of a gasoline engine is to
    A. indicate the temperature of the cooling water
    B. control water flow so as to prevent excessive pressure in the radiator
    C. prevent overheating of the cooling water
    D. prevent circulation of the cooling water when the engine is cold

14. Of the following sets of items, the BEST one to use to clean and adjust ignition points is
    A. crescent wrench, V-block, and sandpaper
    B. screwdriver, feeler gauge, and point file
    C. scraper, micrometer, and sandpaper
    D. pincers, micrometer, and emery cloth

15. The MAIN reason for not allowing oily rags to accumulate in storage closets is that
    A. a rancid odor will develop near the closet
    B. the closet will look messy
    C. oil will drip onto the floor
    D. a fire may start by spontaneous combustion

16. A certain paint can cover 310 square feet per gallon. The number of gallons of this paint required to paint 200 lines each 6 inches wide and 18 feet, 6 inches long is MOST nearly
    A. 2 B. 4 C. 6 D. 8

17. Paint brushes that are used with an oil-based paint are usually cleaned with
    A. turpentine B. linseed oil C. acetone D. alcohol

18. Assume that, while you are using an electric drill with a long electric cord, the drill suddenly stops operating. Of the following, the FIRST thing that you should do is to
    A. remove the casing of the drill to see whether the insulation of the armature is damaged
    B. check whether the cord is still plugged into the outlet
    C. check the fuses in the supply circuit
    D. inspecft the cord for a broken wire

18.____

19. A cold chisel with a "mushroomed" head is properly "dressed" by
    A. filing the cutting edge
    B. heating the head until it is red hot and quenching it in oil
    C. grinding off the turned over material
    D. heating the head of the chisel until it is red hot and, after letting it cool slowly, tapping it until all the chips fall off

19.____

20. Of the following sets of items, the BEST one to use to clean and adjust ignition points is
    A. crescent wrench, V-block, and sandpaper
    B. screwdriver, feeler gauge, and point file
    C. scraper, micrometer, and sandpaper
    D. pincers, micrometer, and emery cloth

20.____

KEY (CORRECT ANSWERS)

1.	A	11.	B
2.	D	12.	B
3.	A	13.	D
4.	C	14.	B
5.	B	15.	D
6.	B	16.	C
7.	D	17.	A
8.	B	18.	B
9.	A	19.	C
10.	A	20.	B

TEST 3

DIRECTIONS: Each question or incomplete statement is followed by several suggested answers or completions. Select the one that BEST answers the question or completes the statement. *PRINT THE LETTER OF THE CORRECT ANSWER IN THE SPACE AT THE RIGHT.*

1. Assume that, while you are using an electric drill with a long electric cord, the drill suddenly stops operating. Of the following, the FIRST thing that you should do is to
    A. remove the casing of the drill to see whether the insulation of the armature is damaged
    B. check whether the cord is still plugged into the outlet
    C. check the fuses in the supply circuit
    D. inspect the cord for a broken wire

    1.____

2. A cold chisel with a "mushroomed" head is PROPERLY "dressed" by
    A. filing the cutting edge
    B. heating the head until it is red hot and quenching it in oil
    C. grinding off the turned over material
    D. heating the head of the chisel until it is red hot and, after letting it cool slowly, tapping it until all the chips fall off

    2.____

3. A pipe reamer is used to
    A. thread pipe
    B. enlarge the size of a pipe
    C. remove burrs from the inside of a pipe
    D. join pipes of different sizes

    3.____

4. Where only a short swing of the handle is possible, the BEST tool to use to tighten a nut or bolt is the _____ wrench.
    A. Stillson   B. open end   C. monkey   D. ratchet

    4.____

5. The wrench which is used on set screws is COMMONLY called the _____ wrench.
    A. torque   B. Allen   C. Stillson   D. Crescent

    5.____

6. A box wrench is BEST used on
    A. Allen screws   B. pipe fittings
    C. hexagonal nuts   D. knurled thumb screws

    6.____

7. The BEST screwdriver to use when driving screws in close quarters is the
    A. butt   B. angled   C. Phillips   D. offset

    7.____

8. A "12-24" screw is MOST likely a _____ screw.
    A. machine   b. sheet metal   C. lag   D. wood

    8.____

9. The one of the following fasteners which is threaded at both ends is the
   A. lag screw　　　　　　　　　B. stud
   C. bolt　　　　　　　　　　　　D. machine screw

10. Tips of masonry drills are USUALLY made of
    A. carbide　　B. corundum　　C. mild steel　　D. beryllium

11. A 5-inch length of pipe with male threads at each end is called a
    A. stud　　　B. coupling　　C. sleeve　　D. nipple

12. Grade No. 2 sandpaper is
    A. finer than grade 1/0　　　B. coarser than grade 3
    C. finer than grade 2/0　　　D. coarser than grade 1

13. The one of the following lists of materials which includes ALL of the ingredients of concrete is cement,
    A. gravel, and water　　　　B. lime, sand, and water
    C. sand, gravel, and water　　D. sand, and water

14. The MAIN purpose of the tool known as a file card is to _____ files.
    A. clean　　　　　　　　　　B. sort out
    C. prevent damage to　　　　D. sharpen

15. The pull exerted by a man lifting a 200 lb. load by means of a four-part block and fall, ignoring friction, is _____ lbs.
    A. 100　　　B. 75　　　C. 50　　　D. 25

16. Of the following, turpentine is a solvent for
    A. shellac　　　　　　　　　B. latex paint
    C. calcimine　　　　　　　　D. red lead paint

17. In a truck's gasoline engine, the condenser is a part of the
    A. distributor　　　　　　　B. cooling system
    C. power take off　　　　　D. fuel system

18. Pneumatic tools are operated by a(n)
    A. air compressor　　　　　B. Pelton wheel
    C. Archimedean screw　　　D. hydraulic ram

19. The gauge on the tank of an air compressor measures
    A. temperature of air in the tank　　B. pressure of air in the tank
    C. humidity of the atmosphere　　　D. barometric pressure

20. A paint sprayer may have gauges showing the pressure of the tank, the paint pressure, and the atomizer pressure. When the sprayer is operating properly, the

    A. paint pressure is higher than the tank pressure
    B. atomizer pressure is higher than the tank pressure
    C. paint and atomizer pressures are equal
    D. atomizer pressure is higher than the paint pressure

20.____

KEY (CORRECT ANSWERS)

1.	B	11.	D
2.	C	12.	D
3.	C	13.	C
4.	D	14.	A
5.	B	15.	C
6.	C	16.	D
7.	D	17.	A
8.	A	18.	A
9.	B	19.	B
10.	A	20.	D

EXAMINATION SECTION
TEST 1

DIRECTIONS: Each question or incomplete statement is followed by several suggested answers or completions. Select the one that BEST answers the question or completes the statement. *PRINT THE LETTER OF THE CORRECT ANSWER IN THE SPACE AT THE RIGHT.*

1. Subordinates do NOT object to strict regulations if they

    A. believe the supervisor approves of the regulation
    B. apply only to minor phases of the work
    C. are enforced without bias and favor
    D. result in improved departmental procedures

    1.____

2. When a supervisor observes one employee gossip about the work of another, he should

    A. ask for such accusations to be made in writing and in front of the man accused
    B. inform the former that his ideas about the work of another employee should be kept to himself
    C. let the two employees straighten out the matter privately and peacefully
    D. make note of the remarks to use in the future against either of the two employees

    2.____

3. A supervisor who notices that two of his sanitation men are always quarreling should

    A. ask the District Superintendent to bring up on charges the one he thinks responsible
    B. let them work out their own problems as they work side by side
    C. reprimand the man he thinks responsible at a roll call
    D. separate them by assigning them to different areas of work

    3.____

4. Of the following, the MAJOR responsibility of a supervisor is to

    A. create an attitude in his men receptive to departmental policy
    B. get the work of his section done properly
    C. make himself liked and respected by his men
    D. see that all his men are assigned work impartially

    4.____

5. In establishing a new policy, a supervisor should FIRST

    A. announce the policy at roll call and warn that the assistant supervisor will enforce it strictly
    B. discuss the policy with the assistant supervisor and get his ideas on how to carry out this policy
    C. talk with each man individually to show him how this policy will affect him
    D. tell the men he is sorry for the change, but disclaim all responsibility for it

    5.____

6. Assume that you are appointed supervisor of a section where there are two assistant supervisors who have been with the department longer than yourself and are on the list for supervisor. The MOST appropriate technique for you to use in handling this situation is to

    6.____

A. ask the district supervisor to warn these assistant supervisors that you are in full charge
B. call them aside your first day and warn them that you are in full charge
C. show them that you are in charge immediately by being a tough supervisor
D. treat them as you do all the rest but consult them about matters that they are well informed on

7. A supervisor can get his men to follow his directions MOST easily if he 7.____

   A. asks the men to remember that following orders is a factor in service rating
   B. explains the reasons for these directions
   C. tells them that it is for the good of the department
   D. warns them of the penalty for not following them

8. A supervisor learns that one of his best men wishes to transfer to another kind of work. 8.____
Of the following, the MOST appropriate action for the supervisor to take is to

   A. ask the other men in the section if anything is wrong with present working conditions
   B. discuss with the man the disadvantages of the kind of work he is interested in
   C. find out if any personal problems have arisen that make a transfer desirable
   D. help the man locate another job with another division of the department

9. A supervisor who is "breaking in" a new man should 9.____

   A. carefully explain the work to the man as he takes him around
   B. explain what should not be done rather than what should be done
   C. show the man where he works and let him begin
   D. tell the man the faults of all the other men in the section

10. A supervisor who feels that a probationary sanitation man is doing below average work 10.____
should FIRST

    A. advise the man to look for a transfer to another department
    B. decide whether there is a cause for this kind of performance which can be cured
    C. lower the standards that have been set for this job
    D. recommend to the superintendent that the man be let go at the end of the probationary period

11. A supervisor who finds that a few men who are ordinarily capable are having difficulties 11.____
with their regular assignments should

    A. build up their morale by praising their past performances
    B. report them to the superintendent for disciplinary action
    C. talk to them about their assignments and iron out any problems
    D. warn them that they will receive poor service ratings

12. A new supervisor who wishes to gain the cooperation of his men should 12.____

    A. be cooperative in all his dealings with his men
    B. criticize the administration's policies
    C. make a strong demand for cooperation
    D. threaten them with poor service ratings

3 (#1)

13. A taxpayer uses abusive language in complaining to a supervisor about the collection service he receives from the men who service his neighborhood.
 Of the following, the procedure for the supervisor to follow is to

 A. agree with everything he says to calm him down, but do nothing because of his attitude
 B. give him a lecture on how to influence people to do what he wants them to do
 C. listen to what he has to say and explain what can be done to correct the situation
 D. tell the taxpayer city employees do not have to take this kind of abuse

13.____

14. A new supervisor who wishes to gain the respect of his men should make decisions

 A. after consulting his men for their opinions
 B. only after considering all the available information
 C. quickly and stick to them whether right or wrong
 D. quickly and change them if they are wrong

14.____

15. A taxpayer complains to a supervisor that a sanitation man has acted in a rude way when collecting garbage.
 Of the following, the supervisor should

 A. discuss the matter with the employee, pointing out that it gives the department bad press
 B. ignore the matter since it probably will not occur again
 C. tell the sanitation man that he must not offend taxpayers since they support the city
 D. warn the employee and tell him a repetition may cause dismissal

15.____

16. A supervisor of a section realizes that he has inadvertently given an unknown telephone caller incorrect information on a departmental procedure.
 Of the following, he should

 A. call the man back at once and give him the correct information
 B. discuss the matter with his superintendent and clarify the procedure to prevent future mistakes
 C. inform Central Office to correct the information if the man calls anywhere in the department
 D. send an official communication on departmental stationery giving the correct facts

16.____

17. A new sanitation man reports to his supervisor that he has made a minor error in performing a task. This is the first time this man has made such an error.
 The PROPER procedure for the supervisor to follow is to

 A. help the man correct the error explaining how to avoid such errors in the future
 B. report the man to the District Superintendent for disciplinary action
 C. reprimand the man very sternly so that this error will not occur again
 D. tell the man not to worry since it was only a minor error

17.____

18. A supervisor who does not know the answer to a problem raised by a man under his supervision should

 A. act as if he knew the solution and make a decision
 B. consult other supervisors and abide by the majority opinion

18.____

C. suggest that the man use his ingenuity in solving new situations
D. work together with the man towards a solution after admitting he does not know the answer

19. A supervisor who has to inform one of his men that his work is *unsatisfactory* should

    A. ask another employee to hint to the man that his work is getting unfavorable comment
    B. be angry when doing so in order to impress the man
    C. inform him at morning roll call so that the man will do a good job that day
    D. point out some good attributes so that the man will be encouraged to try harder

20. A supervisor who sees one of his men make an error in performing a task should

    A. call the man aside and point out the error in a way which will not cause resentment
    B. correct the work himself and later when the men are together point out the error in a pleasant way
    C. do nothing until the next roll call when he can reprimand the man about his work
    D. do nothing but watch the man's work more carefully in the future

21. When it becomes necessary to take disciplinary action, a wise supervisor should

    A. do nothing but rely on the other men to penalize the man involved
    B. let the employee decide what action should be taken
    C. know what the usual procedure should be in such cases
    D. shift the responsibility lor action to his superiors in the department

22. A supervisor who is training a new man for the job should FIRST

    A. explain all the details of the Department of Sanitation procedures
    B. find out what the man already knows about the job
    C. give the man a pep talk on the advantages of the job
    D. put the man to work and let him learn by doing

23. A supervisor notices that one of his men who is very efficient always complains about the work to be done. This complaining is having a bad effect on the other men. Of the following, the BEST action to take is to

    A. arrange for the man to have more work to do so that he hasn't any time to complain
    B. give the man special assignments so that he loses the reason for his complaints
    C. talk to the man privately and try to effect a change in his attitude
    D. talk to the other men and ask them to ignore his complaints because he is so efficient

24. Of the following, the attribute which contributes MOST to leadership is the ability to

    A. get respect from others
    B. make people fear you
    C. mix well with others
    D. smile under all circumstances

25. Of the following, the MOST important quality for a good supervisor to have is 25.____

    A. the ability to handle men
    B. an imposing appearance to impress the men
    C. a neat appearance to set himself up as a model
    D. skill in writing required reports

26. Of the following, the BEST way for a supervisor to keep the respect of his men is to 26.____

    A. approve and praise all work performed
    B. be fair in all his dealings with subordinates
    C. get the men to do more work by means of contests
    D. offer criticism and suggestions for each job done

27. Assume that you, as a supervisor, have issued a warning concerning an offense to a building superintendent and you have advised and instructed him in how to correct the offense. On following up after a reasonable time, you find the situation has not been corrected and the offender does not intend to correct it.
    The PROPER procedure for you to follow is to 27.____

    A. discuss the matter with other supervisors and take the best advice you get
    B. have a patrolman order the superintendent to remedy the situation
    C. have some sanitation men correct the situation and bill the superintendent for the Work done
    D. have the superintendent summoned to appear in Municipal Term of Magistrate's Court

28. A supervisor who has been with the department for many years is assigned a newly appointed assistant supervisor who attempts to take over the supervision of the section.
    Of the following, the BEST action for the supervisor to take is to 28.____

    A. inform the assistant supervisor that he, the supervisor, is responsible for the section
    B. inform the assistant supervisor of those matters which are his responsibility and those retained by the supervisor
    C. tell the assistant supervisor that the section has functioned smoothly without his assistance
    D. tell the sanitation men to take orders only from the supervisor

29. Of the following, the MOST important requirement for the supervisor of a section is that he 29.____

    A. collect more garbage than any of his subordinates
    B. keep efficient working relationships with his men, his superiors and the public
    C. keep records of all problems that arise in his section
    D. help plan new equipment to improve departmental conditions

30. In supervising waste collections, the factor LEAST likely to contribute to delays in schedules is the

    A. inclement weather
    B. lesser output of material increasing time to gather a load
    C. mechanical failure of collection trucks
    D. necessity for daily or tri-weekly collections

KEY (CORRECT ANSWERS)

1.	C	11.	C	21.	C
2.	B	12.	A	22.	B
3.	D	13.	C	23.	C
4.	B	14.	B	24.	A
5.	B	15.	A	25.	A
6.	D	16.	B	26.	B
7.	B	17.	A	27.	D
8.	C	18.	D	28.	B
9.	A	19.	D	29.	B
10.	B	20.	A	30.	D

TEST 2

DIRECTIONS: Each question or incomplete statement is followed by several suggested answers or completions. Select the one that BEST answers the question or completes the statement. *PRINT THE LETTER OF THE CORRECT ANSWER IN THE SPACE AT THE RIGHT.*

1. All authorities on safety claim that accidents do not just happen. According to this statement, it follows that

   A. accidents result from the deliberate intention to do damage
   B. an accident is the result of a coincidence
   C. every accident has a definite cause
   D. it would be possible to eliminate accidents entirely

   1.____

2. A supervisor who has instructed his men in safety measures has a driver who got hurt as a result of violating a safety rule six months after the instruction period. Of the following, the CORRECT procedure to follow is to

   A. assume that since the instructions were given originally, that should be sufficient
   B. caution drivers working under dangerous conditions continually
   C. reprimand the driver since the man should be responsible for his own safety
   D. understand the driver's attitude since other drivers probably also ignore safety rules

   2.____

3. Records have been kept by insurance companies showing that when a supervisor who has a good safety record goes into another plant of his own company which previously had not had as good a safety record, he is able by his supervision to bring down the number of accidents in that plant. It has also been found that supervisors who were not good on safety when transferred to another plant which had a good record were not able to maintain good safety standards.
   According to this paragraph

   A. a supervisor with a good safety record if put in a plant with a bad safety record has more work to do
   B. a foreman with a bad safety record on moving to a plant with a good safety record can take it easy
   C. safety-minded supervisors make their influence felt among their subordinates
   D. the safety record in one plant is not related to the record in another plant

   3.____

4. Of the following instructions relative to safety, the one which is NOT the specific duty of the supervisor to enforce is:

   A. Always sweep against traffic.
   B. Do not back up without proper guidance.
   C. Do not bear out from the curb in a truck without signalling.
   D. Get a truck to replace a damaged one.

   4.____

5. In administering first aid to the victim of an accident who is suffering from more than one of the following conditions, you should treat FIRST for

   A. asphyxiation
   B. fractured bones

   5.____

C. poisoning
D. profuse arterial bleeding

6. In treating a deep cut in the leg which results in severe bleeding, the FIRST procedure to follow is to

   A. apply a tourniquet between the wound and the heart
   B. apply digital pressure directly on the cut
   C. give the patient a strong stimulant
   D. keep the victim in a prone position, head elevated

7. A laborer has cut a small gash in his leg on the edge of a jagged timber. Of the following, the BEST one to use directly on the wound is

   A. adhesive tape   B. collodion
   C. friction tape   D. a sterile gauze pad

8. Of the following, the one which is NOT used to control bleeding is

   A. cold applications   B. digital pressure
   C. hot applications   D. tourniquets

9. Of the following statements concerning safety precaution in a garage, the LEAST accurate is:

   A. All machinery for cutting, drilling and charging should have the proper safeguards attached.
   B. Better lighting will often eliminate dangerous working positions.
   C. Hazardous conditions should be corrected as soon as they are discovered.
   D. Principles of accident prevention differ in small, as compared with large, garages.

10. Concerning accidents, the MOST accurate statement is:

    A. All individuals are equally prone to have accidents.
    B. It is probable that most of the accidents occur to the same few persons in any one group.
    C. Pessimistic people tend to be more careful and so have fewer accidents.
    D. Physiological and psychological factors have little effect on the control of accidents.

11. Of the following methods of cleaning grease and oil from slippery floors, the LEAST desirable is to

    A. clean the grease off the floor by washing with gasoline
    B. cover the floor with air slack lime, allow it to remain for several hours and then scrape the floor
    C. scrape the floor and remove grease with caustic soda or potash
    D. sprinkle common sand and leave on the floor for a while, then use a stiff broom to sweep away

12. Of the following statements concerning a carbon dioxide extinguisher, the LEAST accurate is:

    A. An operator of such equipment needs no safeguards in an unventilated room.
    B. These extinguishers are effective on electrical equipment fires.

C. Such extinguishers do not have to be protected against freezing.
D. These extinguishers should be held so that their discharge is aimed at the base of the flame.

13. A supervisor who is asked by a citizen about the Department of Sanitation's collection procedures of trade wastes should

    A. give the citizen as little information as possible
    B. refer the citizen to the Department's public relations people or to the Commissioner
    C. refuse to discuss the matter since it might concern higher echelons of the Department
    D. tell the citizen as much factual information as possible

14. Of the following, the one which is the LEAST important reason for collecting rubbish is that it

    A. assists in the elimination of fire hazards
    B. helps in the extermination of vermin
    C. prevents health hazards of decayed vegetable matter
    D. rids the city streets of trash piles

15. The BEST reason for the collection of garbage in a city is that it

    A. gives employment to a large number of citizens
    B. helps keep up public health conditions
    C. keeps streets and roads neat and orderly
    D. makes the city beautiful for visitors

16. If a supervisor warns the superintendent of an apartment house to keep the garbage and rubbish separate, he is

    A. being discourteous to the public
    B. creating a bad public relations situation
    C. doing his required duty
    D. making things easier for his sanitation men

17. A supervisor who is investigating a complaint calls on a taxpayer who is very talkative and asks innumerable questions.
    Of the following, the BEST action for the supervisor to take is to

    A. answer the taxpayer as briefly as possible and finish his business as rapidly as possible
    B. interrupt the taxpayer bluntly so that he can finish the department's business
    C. remain patiently until the taxpayer talks himself out
    D. tell the taxpayer that he is not paid to make social visits

18. A homeowner calls a section office to complain that a new garbage can has been damaged by the sanitation men who collect from his home.
    The CORRECT action for a supervisor to take is to tell the homeowner

    A. to buy a new can and present his bill to the Chief Clerk
    B. to inform the Comptroller's Office
    C. that he will investigate the matter
    D. that he will transfer the sanitation men

19. A homeowner must REMOVE empty garbage cans from the sidewalks to the rear of his premises or to the inside of the premises

    A. as soon as they have been emptied
    B. within an hour after they have been emptied
    C. within four hours after they have been emptied
    D. by evening of the day on which they have been emptied

20. A garbage can, according to the Sanitary Code, should be large enough to hold NOT more than _____ cubic feet of material

    A. one   B. two   C. three   D. four

21. Garbage cans are required by the Sanitary Code to be made of

    A. metal
    B. non-transparent plastic
    C. waterproof material
    D. wood

22. Before a supervisor decides who is responsible for a bad situation he should

    A. collect and file all reports
    B. get friendly with the people involved
    C. give people involved copies of the code of discipline
    D. investigate the situation thoroughly

23. Of the following, the MOST acceptable method of treating garbage to prevent odors on incineration is to

    A. have the garbage aerated before using it
    B. keep the temperature in the furnaces at 1250 degrees
    C. store the garbage in airtight bins before using it
    D. wet the garbage before putting it into the furnace

24. A supervisor should know that the LEAST important use the Department of Sanitation has for ashes is to

    A. make fill for landfills
    B. make fuel for incinerators
    C. provide cinders for icy streets
    D. provide clean fills for a dump

25. Of the following complaints made to the supervisor of a Section, the one over which the supervisor has NO jurisdiction is the

    A. damage sanitation men cause to garbage cans
    B. failure of sanitation men to return cans to the proper place on the curb
    C. frequency of collection for different areas of the section
    D. unsanitary garbage arrangements in the kitchen of a luncheonette

26. If a passerby calls the section to report a large dead animal on a street in your section, you should   26._____

   A. have him call the Police Department
   B. refer him to the A.S.P.C.A.
   C. refer him to a private rendering concern
   D. tell him that you will take care of it

27. Of the following reasons, a householder has a LEGITIMATE complaint when she complains that her garbage was not collected if   27._____

   A. the can contained four cubic feet of matter
   B. the can had mixed garbage and trade wastes
   C. a snow storm prevented regular collections
   D. it was in its proper place when the truck passed

28. When a homeowner complains that his garbage has not been collected on the collection day for his address, he should be told that it is his responsibility if   28._____

   A. less than four cans were set out
   B. more than ten cans were put out
   C. the truck skipped his house accidentally
   D. it was not put out at the proper time

29. In the destructor method of garbage disposal, the LEAST necessary of the following requirements as to the location of the incinerator is that   29._____

   A. it should be centrally located with respect to the population it serves
   B. the site should be large enough so that noise and odors are isolated
   C. the location of the plant should be such as to dissipate possible odors
   D. there should be adequate area for garbage trucks to unload

30. Of the factors listed, the LEAST important in setting up a collection route is the   30._____

   A. average output of household waste
   B. daily weather variations
   C. disposal facilities and their distance from the section
   D. necessity for daily or tri-weekly service

KEY (CORRECT ANSWERS)

1. C	11. A	21. A
2. B	12. A	22. D
3. C	13. D	23. B
4. D	14. C	24. B
5. D	15. B	25. D
6. B	16. C	26. D
7. D	17. A	27. D
8. C	18. C	28. D
9. D	19. A	29. A
10. B	20. B	30. B

TEST 3

DIRECTIONS: Each question or incomplete statement is followed by several suggested answers or completions. Select the one that BEST answers the question or completes the statement. *PRINT THE LETTER OF THE CORRECT ANSWER IN THE SPACE AT THE RIGHT.*

1. In stopping a motor vehicle on snow-covered streets, the OBJECTION to disengaging the clutch and applying the brakes hard at the same time is that

    A. the abuse of tires under such conditions is greater
    B. it causes too great a loss of power
    C. it permits the motor to race which causes overheating
    D. the possibility of skidding is increased

    1.____

2. Of the following, the one *most likely* to cause an automobile motor to overheat is

    A. driving too fast
    B. too much oil in the crankcase
    C. too rich a gas mixture in the carburetor
    D. water circulation partially blocked by sediment

    2.____

3. Of the following practices, the LEAST important in prolonging tire life is to

    A. avoid quick starts and sudden stops
    B. do not strike curbs with tires
    C. have the distributor in clean condition
    D. keep brakes in good even adjustment

    3.____

4. Of the following, the one which is NOT a cause of overheating a motor is

    A. braking friction
    B. broken fan belt
    C. frozen water preventing circulation
    D. lack of water in the radiator

    4.____

5. The mechanism in a motor vehicle which allows it to move around a curve smoothly is the

    A. clutch
    B. differential gear
    C. gear box
    D. universal joint

    5.____

QUESTIONS 6-15.

Listed below in questions 6-15 are various tasks performed by mechanical equipment. In Column II is a list of mechanical equipment. For each item in Column I, select the proper machine in Column II and place the letter preceding that machine next to the corresponding item number of Column I.

2 (#3)

	Column I		Column II	
6.	Clearing intersections and bus stops	A.	collection trucks	6.____
7.	Clearing snow from bridges and highways	B.	crosswalk plows	7.____
8.	Delivering supplies	C.	flushing machines	8.____
9.	Distributing sand and salt	D.	gasoline tank trucks	____
10.	Refueling in field	E.	mechanical brooms	10.____
11.	Hauling refuse	F.	passenger car	11.____
12.	Loading snow into trucks	G.	rotary brooms	12.____
13.	Sweeping pavements	H.	service truck	13.____
		J.	snogo	
14.	Towing purposes	K.	spreaders	14.____
		L.	tractor bulldozer	
15.	Washing pavements	M.	timekeepers	15.____
		N.	wrecker	

QUESTIONS 16-25.

Listed below in questions 16-25 are terms used in the Department of Sanitation. In Column II are listed various definitions. For each item in Column I select the proper definition in Column II.

	Column I		Column II	
16.	Athey wagon	A.	an area along the waterfront where shallow water is being filled in to reclaim the area	16.____
17.	Cross bar	B.	a bar arranged like a fence to keep curious people away from sanitation work	17.____
18.	Hired truck	C.	bars placed over a sewer opening to keep a man from falling in	18.____
19.	Landfill	D.	a department location where trucks bring waste materials to dump into barges for reclamation purposes elsewhere	19.____
		E.	horse drawn vehicle for spreading waste products on fills along the Sound.	

20. Machine flushing	F. measurements of water in a slip	20._____
	G. payroll for employees of other city departments for helping the Department of Sanitation remove snow	
21. Marine unloading plant	H. mechanism for measuring high degrees of heat	21._____
	I. a person who collects and privately disposes of waste materials using his own truck	
22. Private cartman	K. a truck owned privately that is used to help the city dispose of snow	22._____
	L. a swampy or blighted area where material is trucked directly to the area and deposited on ground	
23. Pyrometer	M. the use of the flushing trucks to clean streets generally	23._____
24. Soundings	N. use of large city flushing trucks to remove snow	24._____
25. Waterfront disposal station	O. tractor drawn vehicle used for distributing waste products at fills	25._____

KEY (CORRECT ANSWERS)

1. D
2. D
3. C
4. A
5. B

6. B
7. G
8. H
9. K
10. D

11. A
12. J
13. E
14. N
15. C

16. O
17. C
18. K
19. L
20. M

21. A
22. I
23. H
24. F
25. D

EXAMINATION SECTION
TEST 1

DIRECTIONS: Each question or incomplete statement is foll'owed by several suggested answers or completions. Select the one that BEST answers the question or completes the statement. *PRINT THE LETTER OF THE CORRECT ANSWER IN THE SPACE AT THE RIGHT.*

1. Of the following, the one MOST important quality required of a good supervisor is

    A. ambition
    B. leadership
    C. friendliness
    D. popularity

2. It is often said that a supervisor can delegate authority but **never responsibility**. This means MOST NEARLY that

    A. a supervisor must do his own work if he expects it to be done properly
    B. a supervisor can assign someone else to do his work, but in the last analysis, the supervisor himself must take the blame for any actions followed
    C. authority and responsibility are two separate things that cannot be borne by the same person
    D. it is better for a supervisor never to delegate his authority

3. One of your men who is a habitual complainer asks you to grant him a minor privilege. Before granting or denying such a request, you should consider

    A. the merits of the case
    B. that it is good for group morale to grant a request of this nature
    C. the man's seniority
    D. that to deny such a request will lower your standing with the men

4. A supervisory practice on the part of a foreman which is MOST likely to lead to confusion and inefficiency is for him to

    A. give orders verbally directly to the man assigned to the job
    B. issue orders only in writing
    C. follow up his orders after issuing them
    D. relay his orders to the men through co-workers

5. It would be POOR supervision on a foreman's part if he

    A. asked an experienced maintainer for his opinion on the method of doing a special job
    B. make it a policy to avoid criticizing a man in front of his co-workers
    C. consulted his assistant supervisor on unusual problems
    D. allowed a cooling-off period of several days before giving one of his men a deserved reprimand

6. Of the following behavior characteristics of a supervisor, the one that is MOST likely to lower the morale of the men he supervises is

    A. diligence
    B. favoritism
    C. punctuality
    D. thoroughness

7. Of the following, the BEST method of getting an employee who is not working up to his capacity to produce more work is to

    A. have another employee criticize his production
    B. privately criticize his production but encourage him to produce more
    C. criticize his production before his associates
    D. criticize his production and threaten to fire him

8. Of the following, the BEST thing for a supervisor to do when a subordinate has done a very good job is to

    A. tell him to take it easy
    B. praise his work
    C. reduce his workload
    D. say nothing because he may become conceited

9. Your orders to your crew are MOST likely to be followed if you

    A. explain the reasons for these orders
    B. warn that all violators will be punished
    C. promise easy assignments to those who follow these orders best
    D. say that they are for the good of the department

10. In order to be a good supervisor, you should

    A. impress upon your men that you demand perfection in their work at all times
    B. avoid being blamed for your crew's mistakes
    C. impress your superior with your ability
    D. see to it that your men get what they are entitled to

11. In giving instructions to a crew, you should

    A. speak in as loud a tone as possible
    B. speak in a coaxing, persuasive manner
    C. speak quietly, clearly, and courteously
    D. always use the word *please* when giving instructions

12. Of the following factors, the one which is LEAST important in evaluating an employee and his work is his

    A. dependability   B. quantity of work done
    C. quality of work done D. education and training

13. When a District Superintendent first assumes his command, it is LEAST important for him at the beginning to observe

    A. how his equipment is designed and its adaptability
    B. how to reorganize the district for greater efficiency
    C. the capabilities of the men in the district
    D. the methods of operation being employed

14. When making an inspection of one of the buildings under your supervision, the BEST   14.____
    procedure to follow in making a record of the inspection is to

    A. return immediately to the office and write a report from memory
    B. write down all the important facts during or as soon as you complete the inspection
    C. fix in your mind all important facts so that you can repeat them from memory if necessary
    D. fix in your mind all important facts so that you can make out your report at the end of the day

15. Assume that your superior has directed you to make certain changes in your established   15.____
    procedure. After using this modified procedure on several occasions, you find that the
    original procedure was distinctly superior and you wish to return to it.
    You should

    A. let your superior find this out for himself
    B. simply change back to the original procedure
    C. compile definite data and information to prove your case to your superior
    D. persuade one of the more experienced workers to take this matter up with your superior

16. An inspector visited a large building under construction. He inspected the soil lines at 9   16.____
    M., water lines at 10 A.M., fixtures at 11 A.M., and did his office work in the afternoon. He
    followed the same pattern daily for weeks.
    This procedure was

    A. *good;* because it was methodical and he did not miss anything
    B. *good;* because it gave equal time to all phases of the plumbing
    C. *bad;* because not enough time was devoted to fixtures
    D. *bad;* because the tradesmen knew when the inspection would occur

17. Assume that one of the foremen in a training course, which you are conducting, pro-   17.____
    poses a poor solution for a maintenance problem.
    Of the following, the BEST course of action for you to take is to

    A. accept the solution tentatively and correct it during the next class meeting
    B. point out all the defects of this proposed solution and wait until somebody thinks of a better solution
    C. try to get the class to reject this proposed solution and develop a better solution
    D. let the matter pass since somebody will present a better solution as the class work proceeds

18. As a supervisor, you should be seeking ways to improve the efficiency of shop operations   18.____
    by means such as changing established work procedures.
    The following are offered as possible actions that you should consider in changing
    established work procedures:
        I. Make changes only when your foremen agree to them
        II. Discuss changes with your supervisor before putting them into practice
        III. Standardize any operation which is performed on a continuing basis
        IV. Make changes quickly and quietly in order to avoid dissent
        V. Secure expert guidance before instituting unfamiliar procedures

Of the following suggested answers, the one that describes the actions to be taken to change established work procedures is

A. I, IV, and V *only*
B. II, III, and V *only*
C. III, IV, and V *only*
D. All of the above

19. A supervisor determined that a foreman, without informing his superior, delegated responsibility for checking time cards to a member of his gang. The supervisor then called the foreman into his office where he reprimanded the foreman.
    This action of the supervisor in reprimanding the foreman was

    A. *proper;* because the checking of time cards is the foreman's responsibility and should not be delegated
    B. *proper;* because the foreman did not ask the supervisor for permission to delegate responsibility
    C. *improper;* because the foreman may no longer take the initiative in solving future problems
    D. *improper;* because the supervisor is interfering in a function which is not his responsibility

19.____

20. A capable supervisor should check all operations under his control.
    Of the following, the LEAST important reason for doing this is to make sure that

    A. operations are being performed as scheduled
    B. he personally observes all operations at all times
    C. all the operations are still needed
    D. his manpower is being utilized efficiently

20.____

21. A supervisor makes it a practice to apply fair and firm discipline in all cases of rule infractions, including those of a minor nature.
    This practice should PRIMARILY be considered

    A. *bad;* since applying discipline for minor violations is a waste of time
    B. *good;* because not applying discipline for minor infractions can lead to a more serious erosion of discipline
    C. *bad;* because employees do not like to be disciplined for minor violations of the rules
    D. *good;* because violating any rule can cause a dangerous situation to occur

21.____

22. A maintainer would PROPERLY consider it poor supervisory practice for a foreman to consult with him on

    A. which of several repair jobs should be scheduled first
    B. how to cope with personal problems at home
    C. whether the neatness of his headquarters can be improved
    D. how to express a suggestion which the maintainer plans to submit formally

22.____

23. Assume that you have determined that the work of one of your foremen and the men he supervises is consistently behind schedule. When you discuss this situation with the foreman, he tells you that his men are poor workers and then complains that he must spend all of his time checking on their work.
The following actions are offered for your consideration as possible ways of solving the problem of poor performance of the foreman and his men:
   I. Review the work standards with the foreman and determine whether they are realistic
   II. Tell the foreman that you will recommend him for the foreman's training course for retraining
   III. Ask the foreman for the names of the maintainers and then replace them as soon as possible
   IV. Tell the foreman that you expect him to meet a satisfactory level of performance
   V. Tell the foreman to insist that his men work overtime to catch up to the schedule
   VI. Tell the foreman to review the type and amount of training he has given the maintainers
   VII. Tell the foreman that he will be out of a job if he does not produce on schedule
   VIII. Avoid all criticism of the foreman and his methods

Which of the following suggested answers CORRECTLY lists the proper actions to be taken to solve the problem of poor performance of the foreman and his men?

   A. I, II, IV, and VI *only*
   B. I, III, V, and VII *only*
   C. II, III, VI, and VIII *only*
   D. IV, V, VI, and VIII *only*

24. When a conference or a group discussion is tending to turn into a *bull session* without constructive purpose, the BEST action to take is to

   A. reprimand the leader of the *bull session*
   B. redirect the discussion to the business at hand
   C. dismiss the meeting and reschedule it for another day
   D. allow the *bull session* to continue

25. Assume that you have been assigned responsibility for a program in which a high production rate is mandatory. From past experience, you know that your foremen do not perform equally well in the various types of jobs given to them.
Which of the following methods should you use in selecting foremen for the specific types of work involved in the program?

   A. Leave the method of selecting foremen to your supervisor
   B. Assign each foreman to the work he does best
   C. Allow each foreman to choose his own job
   D. Assign each foreman to a job which will permit him to improve his own abilities

KEY (CORRECT ANSWERS)

1. B
2. B
3. A
4. D
5. D

6. B
7. B
8. B
9. A
10. D

11. C
12. D
13. B
14. B
15. C

16. D
17. C
18. B
19. A
20. B

21. B
22. A
23. A
24. B
25. B

TEST 2

DIRECTIONS: Each question or incomplete statement is followed by several suggested answers or completions. Select the one that BEST answers the question or completes the statement. *PRINT THE LETTER OF THE CORRECT ANSWER IN THE SPACE AT THE RIGHT.*

1. A foreman who is familiar with modern management principles should know that the one of the following requirements of an administrator which is LEAST important is his ability to

    A. coordinate work
    B. plan, organize, and direct the work under his control
    C. cooperate with others
    D. perform the duties of the employees under his jurisdiction

    1._____

2. When subordinates request his advice in solving problems encountered in their work, a certain chief occasionally answers the request by first asking the subordinate what he thinks should be done.
   This action by the chief is, on the whole,

    A. *desirable* because it stimulates subordinates to give more thought to the solution of problems encountered
    B. *undesirable* because it discourages subordinates from asking questions
    C. *desirable* because it discourages subordinates from asking questions
    D. *undesirable* because it undermines the confidence of subordinates in the ability of their supervisor

    2._____

3. Of the following factors that may be considered by a unit head in dealing with the tardy subordinate, the one which should be given LEAST consideration is the

    A. frequency with which the employee is tardy
    B. effect of the employee's tardiness upon the work of other employees
    C. willingness of the employee to work overtime when necessary
    D. cause of the employee's tardiness

    3._____

4. The MOST important requirement of a good inspectional report is that it should be

    A. properly addressed   B. lengthy
    C. clear and brief   D. spelled correctly

    4._____

5. Building superintendents frequently inquire about departmental inspectional procedures. Of the following, it is BEST to

    A. advise them to write to the department for an official reply
    B. refuse as the inspectional procedure is a restricted matter
    C. briefly explain the procedure to them
    D. avoid the inquiry by changing the subject

    5._____

6. Reprimanding a crew member before other workers is a

    A. *good practice;* the reprimand serves as a warning to the other workers
    B. *bad practice;* people usually resent criticism made in public
    C. *good practice;* the other workers will realize that the supervisor is fair
    D. *bad practice;* the other workers will take sides in the dispute

    6._____

7. Of the following actions, the one which is LEAST likely to promote good work is for the group leader to

   A. praise workers for doing a good job
   B. call attention to the opportunities for promotion for better workers
   C. threaten to recommend discharge of workers who are below standard
   D. put into practice any good suggestion made by crew members

8. A supervisor notices that a member of his crew has skipped a routine step in his job. Of the following, the BEST action for the supervisor to take is to

   A. promptly question the worker about the incident
   B. immediately assign another man to complete the job
   C. bring up the incident the next time the worker asks for a favor
   D. say nothing about the incident but watch the worker carefully in the future

9. Assume you have been told to show a new worker how to operate a piece of equipment. Your FIRST step should be to

   A. ask the worker if he has any questions about the equipment
   B. permit the worker to operate the equipment himself while you carefully watch to prevent damage
   C. demonstrate the operation of the equipment for the worker
   D. have the worker read an instruction booklet on the maintenance of the equipment

10. Whenever a new man was assigned to his crew, the supervisor would introduce him to all other crew members, take him on a tour of the plant, tell him about bus schedules and places to eat.
    This practice is

    A. *good;* the new man is made to feel welcome
    B. *bad;* supervisors should not interfere in personal matters
    C. *good;* the new man knows that he can bring his personal problems to the supervisor
    D. *bad;* work time should not be spent on personal matters

11. The MOST important factor in successful leadership is the ability to

    A. obtain instant obedience to all orders
    B. establish friendly personal relations with crew members
    C. avoid disciplining crew members
    D. make crew members want to do what should be done

12. Explaining the reasons for departmental procedure to workers tends to

    A. waste time which should be used for productive purposes
    B. increase their interest in their work
    C. make them more critical of departmental procedures
    D. confuse them

13. If you want a job done well, do it yourself. For a supervisor to follow this advice would be

    A. *good;* a supervisor is responsible for the work of his crew
    B. *bad;* a supervisor should train his men, not do their work
    C. *good;* a supervisor should be skilled in all jobs assigned to his crew
    D. *bad;* a supervisor loses respect when he works with his hands

14. When a supervisor discovers a mistake in one of the jobs for which his crew is responsible, it is MOST important for him to find out

    A. whether anybody else knows about the mistake
    B. who was to blame for the mistake
    C. how to prevent similar mistakes in the future
    D. whether similar mistakes occurred in the past

15. A supervisor who has to explain a new procedure to his crew should realize that questions from the crew USUALLY show that they

    A. are opposed to the new procedure
    B. are completely confused by the explanation
    C. need more training in the new procedure
    D. are interested in the explanation

16. A good way for a supervisor to retain the confidence of his or her employees is to

    A. say as little as possible
    B. check work frequently
    C. make no promises unless they will be fulfilled
    D. never hesitate in giving an answer to any question

17. Good supervision is ESSENTIALLY a matter of

    A. patience in supervising workers
    B. care in selecting workers
    C. skill in human relations
    D. fairness in disciplining workers

18. It is MOST important for an employee who has been assigned a monotonous task to

    A. perform this task before doing other work
    B. ask another employee to help
    C. perform this task only after all other work has been completed
    D. take measures to prevent mistakes in performing the task

19. One of your employees has violated a minor agency regulation.
    The FIRST thing you should do is

    A. warn the employee that you will have to take disciplinary action if it should happen again
    B. ask the employee to explain his or her actions
    C. inform your supervisor and wait for advice
    D. write a memo describing the incident and place it in the employee's personnel file

20. One of your employees tells you that he feels you give him much more work than the other employees, and he is having trouble meeting your deadlines.
    You should

    A. ask if he has been under a lot of non-work related stress lately
    B. review his recent assignments to determine if he is correct
    C. explain that this is a busy time, but you are dividing the work equally
    D. tell him that he is the most competent employee and that is why he receives more work

    20.____

21. A supervisor assigns one of his crew to complete a portion of a job. A short time later, the supervisor notices that the portion has not been completed.
    Of the following, the BEST way for the supervisor to handle this is to

    A. ask the crew member why he has not completed the assignment
    B. reprimand the crew member for not obeying orders
    C. assign another crew member to complete the assignment
    D. complete the assignment himself

    21.____

22. Suppose that a member of your crew complains that you are *playing favorites* in assigning work.
    Of the following, the BEST method of handling the complaint is to

    A. deny it and refuse to discuss the matter with the worker
    B. take the opportunity to tell the worker what is wrong with his work
    C. ask the worker for examples to prove his point and try to clear up any misunderstanding
    D. promise to be more careful in making assignments in the future

    22.____

23. A member of your crew comes to you with a complaint. After discussing the matter with him, it is clear that you have convinced him that his complaint was not justified.
    At this point, you should

    A. permit him to drop the matter
    B. make him admit his error
    C. pretend to see some justification in his complaint
    D. warn him against making unjustified complaints

    23.____

24. Suppose that a supervisor has in his crew an older man who works rather slowly. In other respects, this man is a good worker; he is seldom absent, works carefully, never loafs, and is cooperative.
    The BEST way for the supervisor to handle this worker is to

    A. try to get him to work faster and less carefully
    B. give him the most disagreeable job
    C. request that he be given special training
    D. permit him to work at his own speed

    24.____

25. Suppose that a member of your crew comes to you with a suggestion he thinks will save time in doing a job. You realize immediately that it won't work.
Under these circumstances, your BEST action would be to

    A. thank the worker for the suggestion and forget about it
    B. explain to the worker why you think it won't work
    C. tell the worker to put the suggestion in writing
    D. ask the other members of your crew to criticize the suggestion

25.____

KEY (CORRECT ANSWERS)

1.	D	11.	D
2.	A	12.	B
3.	C	13.	B
4.	C	14.	C
5.	C	15.	D
6.	B	16.	C
7.	C	17.	C
8.	A	18.	D
9.	C	19.	B
10.	A	20.	B

21. A
22. C
23. A
24. D
25. B

PHILOSOPHY, PRINCIPLES, PRACTICES AND TECHNICS OF SUPERVISION, ADMINISTRATION, MANAGEMENT AND ORGANIZATION

TABLE OF CONTENTS

		Page
I.	MEANING OF SUPERVISION	1
II.	THE OLD AND THE NEW SUPERVISION	1
III.	THE EIGHT (8) BASIC PRINCIPLES OF THE NEW SUPERVISION	1
	1. Principle of Responsibility	1
	2. Principle of Authority	2
	3. Principle of Self-Growth	2
	4. Principle of Individual Worth	2
	5. Principle of Creative Leadership	2
	6. Principle of Success and Failure	2
	7. Principle of Science	3
	8. Principle of Cooperation	3
IV.	WHAT IS ADMINISTRATION?	3
	1. Practices commonly classed as "Supervisory"	3
	2. Practices commonly classed as "Administrative"	3
	3. Practices classified as both "Supervisory" and "Administrative"	4
V.	RESPONSIBILITIES OF THE SUPERVISOR	4
VI.	COMPETENCIES OF THE SUPERVISOR	4
VII.	THE PROFESSIONAL SUPERVISOR—EMPLOYEE RELATIONSHIP	4
VIII.	MINI-TEXT IN SUPERVISION, ADMINISTRATION, MANAGEMENT AND ORGANIZATION	5
	A. Brief Highlights	5
	1. Levels of Management	5
	2. What the Supervisor Must Learn	6
	3. A Definition of Supervision	6
	4. Elements of the Team Concept	6
	5. Principles of Organization	6
	6. The Four Important Parts of Every Job	6
	7. Principles of Delegation	6
	8. Principles of Effective Communications	7
	9. Principles of Work Improvement	7

TABLE OF CONTENTS (CONTINUED)

10. Areas of Job Improvement	7
11. Seven Key Points in Making Improvements	7
12. Corrective Techniques for Job Improvement	7
13. A Planning Checklist	8
14. Five Characteristics of Good Directions	8
15. Types of Directions	8
16. Controls	8
17. Orienting the New Employee	8
18. Checklist for Orienting New Employees	8
19. Principles of Learning	9
20. Causes of Poor Performance	9
21. Four Major Steps in On-The-Job Instructions	9
22. Employees Want Five Things	9
23. Some Don'ts in Regard to Praise	9
24. How to Gain Your Workers' Confidence	9
25. Sources of Employee Problems	9
26. The Supervisor's Key to Discipline	10
27. Five Important Processes of Management	10
28. When the Supervisor Fails to Plan	10
29. Fourteen General Principles of Management	10
30. Change	10

B. Brief Topical Summaries — 11
- I. Who/What is the Supervisor? — 11
- II. The Sociology of Work — 11
- III. Principles and Practices of Supervision — 12
- IV. Dynamic Leadership — 12
- V. Processes for Solving Problems — 12
- VI. Training for Results — 13
- VII. Health, Safety and Accident Prevention — 13
- VIII. Equal Employment Opportunity — 13
- IX. Improving Communications — 14
- X. Self-Development — 14
- XI. Teaching and Training — 14
  - A. The Teaching Process — 14
    1. Preparation — 14
    2. Presentation — 15
    3. Summary — 15
    4. Application — 15
    5. Evaluation — 15
  - B. Teaching Methods — 15
    1. Lecture — 15
    2. Discussion — 15
    3. Demonstration — 16
    4. Performance — 16
    5. Which Method to Use — 16

PHILOSOPHY, PRINCIPLES, PRACTICES, AND TECHNICS
OF
SUPERVISION, ADMINISTRATION, MANAGEMENT AND ORGANIZATION

I. MEANING OF SUPERVISION

The extension of the democratic philosophy has been accompanied by an extension in the scope of supervision. Modern leaders and supervisors no longer think of supervision in the narrow sense of being confined chiefly to visiting employees, supplying materials, or rating the staff. They regard supervision as being intimately related to all the concerned agencies of society, they speak of the supervisor's function in terms of "growth", rather than the "improvement," of employees.

This modern concept of supervision may be defined as follows:

Supervision is leadership and the development of leadership within groups which are cooperatively engaged in inspection, research, training, guidance and evaluation.

II. THE OLD AND THE NEW SUPERVISION

TRADITIONAL
1. Inspection
2. Focused on the employee
3. Visitation
4. Random and haphazard
5. Imposed and authoritarian
6. One person usually

MODERN
1. Study and analysis
2. Focused on aims, materials, methods, supervisors, employees, environment
3. Demonstrations, intervisitation, workshops, directed reading, bulletins, etc.
4. Definitely organized and planned (scientific)
5. Cooperative and democratic
6. Many persons involved (creative)

III THE EIGHT (8) BASIC PRINCIPLES OF THE NEW SUPERVISION

1. PRINCIPLE OF RESPONSIBILITY
Authority to act and responsibility for acting must be joined.
  a. If you give responsibility, give authority.
  b. Define employee duties clearly.
  c. Protect employees from criticism by others.
  d. Recognize the rights as well as obligations of employees.
  e. Achieve the aims of a democratic society insofar as it is possible within the area of your work.
  f. Establish a situation favorable to training and learning.
  g. Accept ultimate responsibility for everything done in your section, unit, office, division, department.
  h. Good administration and good supervision are inseparable.

2. PRINCIPLE OF AUTHORITY
The success of the supervisor is measured by the extent to which the power of authority is not used.
- a. Exercise simplicity and informality in supervision.
- b. Use the simplest machinery of supervision.
- c. If it is good for the organization as a whole, it is probably justified.
- d. Seldom be arbitrary or authoritative.
- e. Do not base your work on the power of position or of personality.
- f. Permit and encourage the free expression of opinions.

3. PRINCIPLE OF SELF-GROWTH
The success of the supervisor is measured by the extent to which, and the speed with which, he is no longer needed.
- a. Base criticism on principles, not on specifics.
- b. Point out higher activities to employees.
- c. Train for self-thinking by employees, to meet new situations.
- d. Stimulate initiative, self-reliance and individual responsibility.
- e. Concentrate on stimulating the growth of employees rather than on removing defects.

4. PRINCIPLE OF INDIVIDUAL WORTH
Respect for the individual is a paramount consideration in supervision.
- a. Be human and sympathetic in dealing with employees.
- b. Don't nag about things to be done.
- c. Recognize the individual differences among employees and seek opportunities to permit best expression of each personality.

5. PRINCIPLE OF CREATIVE LEADERSHIP
The best supervision is that which is not apparent to the employee.
- a. Stimulate, don't drive employees to creative action.
- b. Emphasize doing good things.
- c. Encourage employees to do what they do best.
- d. Do not be too greatly concerned with details of subject or method.
- e. Do not be concerned exclusively with immediate problems and activities.
- f. Reveal higher activities and make them both desired and maximally possible.
- g. Determine procedures in the light of each situation but see that these are derived from a sound basic philosophy.
- h. Aid, inspire and lead so as to liberate the creative spirit latent in all good employees.

6. PRINCIPLE OF SUCCESS AND FAILURE
There are no unsuccessful employees, only unsuccessful supervisors who have failed to give proper leadership.
- a. Adapt suggestions to the capacities, attitudes, and prejudices of employees.
- b. Be gradual, be progressive, be persistent.
- c. Help the employee find the general principle; have the employee apply his own problem to the general principle.
- d. Give adequate appreciation for good work and honest effort.
- e. Anticipate employee difficulties and help to prevent them.
- f. Encourage employees to do the desirable things they will do anyway.
- g. Judge your supervision by the results it secures.

7. PRINCIPLE OF SCIENCE

Successful supervision is scientific, objective, and experimental. It is based on facts, not on prejudices.

    a. Be cumulative in results.
    b. Never divorce your suggestions from the goals of training.
    c. Don't be impatient of results.
    d. Keep all matters on a professional, not a personal level.
    e. Do not be concerned exclusively with immediate problems and activities.
    f. Use objective means of determining achievement and rating where possible.

8. PRINCIPLE OF COOPERATION

Supervision is a cooperative enterprise between supervisor and employee.

    a. Begin with conditions as they are.
    b. Ask opinions of all involved when formulating policies.
    c. Organization is as good as its weakest link.
    d. Let employees help to determine policies and department programs.
    e. Be approachable and accessible - physically and mentally.
    f. Develop pleasant social relationships.

IV. WHAT IS ADMINISTRATION?

Administration is concerned with providing the environment, the material facilities, and the operational procedures that will promote the maximum growth and development of supervisors and employees. (Organization is an aspect, and a concomitant, of administration.)

There is no sharp line of demarcation between supervision and administration; these functions are intimately interrelated and, often, overlapping. They are complementary activities.

1. PRACTICES COMMONLY CLASSED AS "SUPERVISORY"

    a. Conducting employees conferences
    b. Visiting sections, units, offices, divisions, departments
    c. Arranging for demonstrations
    d. Examining plans
    e. Suggesting professional reading
    f. Interpreting bulletins
    g. Recommending in-service training courses
    h. Encouraging experimentation
    i. Appraising employee morale
    j. Providing for intervisitation

2. PRACTICES COMMONLY CLASSIFIED AS "ADMINISTRATIVE"

    a. Management of the office
    b. Arrangement of schedules for extra duties
    c. Assignment of rooms or areas
    d. Distribution of supplies
    e. Keeping records and reports
    f. Care of audio-visual materials
    g. Keeping inventory records
    h. Checking record cards and books
    i. Programming special activities
    j. Checking on the attendance and punctuality of employees

3. *PRACTICES COMMONLY CLASSIFIED AS BOTH "SUPERVISORY" AND "ADMINISTRATIVE"*
   a. Program construction
   b. Testing or evaluating outcomes
   c. Personnel accounting
   d. Ordering instructional materials

V. RESPONSIBILITIES OF THE SUPERVISOR

A person employed in a supervisory capacity must constantly be able to improve his own efficiency and ability. He represents the employer to the employees and only continuous self-examination can make him a capable supervisor.

Leadership and training are the supervisor's responsibility. An efficient working unit is one in which the employees work with the supervisor. It is his job to bring out the best in his employees. He must always be relaxed, courteous and calm in his association with his employees. Their feelings are important, and a harsh attitude does not develop the most efficient employees.

VI. COMPETENCIES OF THE SUPERVISOR

1. Complete knowledge of the duties and responsibilities of his position.
2. To be able to organize a job, plan ahead and carry through.
3. To have self-confidence and initiative.
4. To be able to handle the unexpected situation and make quick decisions.
5. To be able to properly train subordinates in the positions they are best suited for.
6. To be able to keep good human relations among his subordinates.
7. To be able to keep good human relations between his subordinates and himself and to earn their respect and trust.

VII. THE PROFESSIONAL SUPERVISOR-EMPLOYEE RELATIONSHIP

There are two kinds of efficiency: one kind is only apparent and is produced in organizations through the exercise of mere discipline; this is but a simulation of the second, or true, efficiency which springs from spontaneous cooperation. If you are a manager, no matter how great or small your responsibility, it is your job, in the final analysis, to create and develop this involuntary cooperation among the people whom you supervise. For, no matter how powerful a combination of money, machines, and materials a company may have, this is a dead and sterile thing without a team of willing, thinking and articulate people to guide it.

The following 21 points are presented as indicative of the exemplary basic relationship that should exist between supervisor and employee:

1. Each person wants to be liked and respected by his fellow employee and wants to be treated with consideration and respect by his superior.
2. The most competent employee will make an error. However, in a unit where good relations exist between the supervisor and his employees, tenseness and fear do not exist. Thus, errors are not hidden or covered up and the efficiency of a unit is not impaired.
3. Subordinates resent rules, regulations, or orders that are unreasonable or unexplained.
4. Subordinates are quick to resent unfairness, harshness, injustices and favoritism.
5. An employee will accept responsibility if he knows that he will be complimented for a job well done, and not too harshly chastised for failure; that his supervisor will check the cause of the failure, and, if it was the supervisor's fault, he will assume the blame therefore. If it was the employee's fault, his supervisor will explain the correct method or means of handling the responsibility.

6. An employee wants to receive credit for a suggestion he has made, that is used. If a suggestion cannot be used, the employee is entitled to an explanation. The supervisor should not say "no" and close the subject.
7. Fear and worry slow up a worker's ability. Poor working environment can impair his physical and mental health. A good supervisor avoids forceful methods, threats and arguments to get a job done.
8. A forceful supervisor is able to train his employees individually and as a team, and is able to motivate them in the proper channels.
9. A mature supervisor is able to properly evaluate his subordinates and to keep them happy and satisfied.
10. A sensitive supervisor will never patronize his subordinates.
11. A worthy supervisor will respect his employees' confidences.
12. Definite and clear-cut responsibilities should be assigned to each executive.
13. Responsibility should always be coupled with corresponding authority.
14. No change should be made in the scope or responsibilities of a position without a definite understanding to that effect on the part of all persons concerned.
15. No executive or employee, occupying a single position in the organization, should be subject to definite orders from more than one source.
16. Orders should never be given to subordinates over the head of a responsible executive. Rather than do this, the officer in question should be supplanted.
17. Criticisms of subordinates should, whoever possible, be made privately, and in no case should a subordinate be criticized in the presence of executives or employees of equal or lower rank.
18. No dispute or difference between executives or employees as to authority or responsibilities should be considered too trivial for prompt and careful adjudication.
19. Promotions, wage changes, and disciplinary action should always be approved by the executive immediately superior to the one directly responsible.
20. No executive or employee should ever be required, or expected, to be at the same time an assistant to, and critic of, another.
21. Any executive whose work is subject to regular inspection should, whever practicable, be given the assistance and facilities necessary to enable him to maintain an independent check of the quality of his work.

VIII. MINI-TEXT IN SUPERVISION, ADMINISTRATION, MANAGEMENT, AND ORGANIZATION

A. BRIEF HIGHLIGHTS

Listed concisely and sequentially are major headings and important data in the field for quick recall and review.

1. *LEVELS OF MANAGEMENT*

Any organization of some size has several levels of management. In terms of a ladder the levels are:

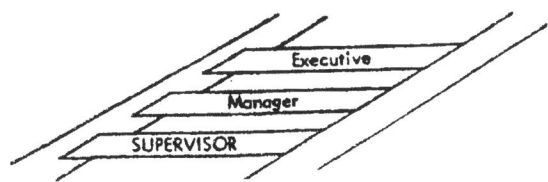

The first level is very important because it is the beginning point of management leadership.

2. WHAT THE SUPERVISOR MUST LEARN

A supervisor must learn to:
(1) Deal with people and their differences
(2) Get the job done through people
(3) Recognize the problems when they exist
(4) Overcome obstacles to good performance
(5) Evaluate the performance of people
(6) Check his own performance in terms of accomplishment

3. A DEFINITION OF SUPERVISOR

The term supervisor means any individual having authority, in the interests of the employer, to hire, transfer, suspend, lay-off, recall, promote, discharge, assign, reward, or discipline other employees or responsibility to direct them, or to adjust their grievances, or effectively to recommend such action, if, in connection with the foregoing, exercise of such authority is not of a merely routine or clerical nature but requires the use of independent judgment.

4. ELEMENTS OF THE TEAM CONCEPT

What is involved in teamwork? The component parts are:

(1) Members   (3) Goals   (5) Cooperation
(2) A leader   (4) Plans   (6) Spirit

5. PRINCIPLES OF ORGANIZATION

(1) A team member must know what his job is.
(2) Be sure that the nature and scope of a job are understood.
(3) Authority and responsibility should be carefully spelled out.
(4) A supervisor should be permitted to make the maximum number of decisions affecting his employees.
(5) Employees should report to only one supervisor.
(6) A supervisor should direct only as many employees as he can handle effectively.
(7) An organization plan should be flexible.
(8) Inspection and performance of work should be separate.
(9) Organizational problems should receive immediate attention.
(10) Assign work in line with ability and experience.

6. THE FOUR IMPORTANT PARTS OF EVERY JOB

(1) Inherent in every job is the *accountability* for results.
(2) A second set of factors in every job is *responsibilities.*
(3) Along with duties and responsibilities one must have the *authority* to act within certain limits without obtaining permission to proceed.
(4) No job exists in a vacuum. The supervisor is surrounded by key *relationships*.

7. PRINCIPLES OF DELEGATION

Where work is delegated for the first time, the supervisor should think in terms of these questions:

(1) Who is best qualified to do this?
(2) Can an employee improve his abilities by doing this?
(3) How long should an employee spend on this?
(4) Are there any special problems for which he will need guidance?
(5) How broad a delegation can I make?

8. PRINCIPLES OF EFFECTIVE COMMUNICATIONS
  (1) Determine the media
  (2) To whom directed?
  (3) Identification and source authority
  (4) Is communication understood?

9. PRINCIPLES OF WORK IMPROVEMENT
  (1) Most people usually do only the work which is assigned to them
  (2) Workers are likely to fit assigned work into the time available to perform it
  (3) A good workload usually stimulates output
  (4) People usually do their best work when they know that results will be reviewed or inspected
  (5) Employees usually feel that someone else is responsible for conditions of work, workplace layout, job methods, type of tools/equipment, and other such factors
  (6) Employees are usually defensive about their job security
  (7) Employees have natural resistance to change
  (8) Employees can support or destroy a supervisor
  (9) A supervisor usually earns the respect of his people through his personal example of diligence and efficiency

10. AREAS OF JOB IMPROVEMENT
The areas of job improvement are quite numerous, but the most common ones which a supervisor can identify and utilize are:

  (1) Departmental layout
  (2) Flow of work
  (3) Workplace layout
  (4) Utilization of manpower
  (5) Work methods
  (6) Materials handling
  (7) Utilization
  (8) Motion economy

11. SEVEN KEY POINTS IN MAKING IMPROVEMENTS
  (1) Select the job to be improved
  (2) Study how it is being done now
  (3) Question the present method
  (4) Determine actions to be taken
  (5) Chart proposed method
  (6) Get approval and apply
  (7) Solicit worker participation

12. CORRECTIVE TECHNIQUES OF JOB IMPROVEMENT

Specific Problems	General Improvement	Corrective Techniques
(1) Size of workload	(1) Departmental layout	(1) Study with scale model
(2) Inability to meet schedules	(2) Flow of work	(2) Flow chart study
(3) Strain and fatigue	(3) Work plan layout	(3) Motion analysis
(4) Improper use of men and skills	(4) Utilization of manpower	(4) Comparison of units produced to standard allowance
(5) Waste, poor quality, unsafe conditions	(5) Work methods	(5) Methods analysis
(6) Bottleneck conditions that hinder output	(6) Materials handling	(6) Flow chart & equipment study
(7) Poor utilization of equipment and machine	(7) Utilization of equipment	(7) Down time vs. running time
(8) Efficiency and productivity of labor	(8) Motion economy	(8) Motion analysis

13. A *PLANNING CHECKLIST*
   - (1) Objectives
   - (2) Controls
   - (3) Delegations
   - (4) Communications
   - (5) Resources
   - (6) Resources
   - (7) Manpower
   - (8) Equipment
   - (9) Supplies and materials
   - (10) Utilization of time
   - (11) Safety
   - (12) Money
   - (13) Work
   - (14) Timing of improvements

14. *FIVE CHARACTERISTICS OF GOOD DIRECTIONS*
   In order to get results, directions must be:
   - (1) Possible of accomplishment
   - (2) Agreeable with worker interests
   - (3) Related to mission
   - (4) Planned and complete
   - (5) Unmistakably clear

15. *TYPES OF DIRECTIONS*
   - (1) Demands or direct orders
   - (2) Requests
   - (3) Suggestion or implication
   - (4) Volunteering

16. *CONTROLS*
   A typical listing of the overall areas in which the supervisor should establish controls might be:
   - (1) Manpower
   - (2) Materials
   - (3) Quality of work
   - (4) Quantity of work
   - (5) Time
   - (6) Space
   - (7) Money
   - (8) Methods

17. *ORIENTING THE NEW EMPLOYEE*
   - (1) Prepare for him
   - (2) Welcome the new employee
   - (3) Orientation for the job
   - (4) Follow-up

18. *CHECKLIST FOR ORIENTING NEW EMPLOYEES*

	Yes	No
(1) Do your appreciate the feelings of new employees when they first report for work?	___	___
(2) Are you aware of the fact that the new employee must make a big adjustment to his job?	___	___
(3) Have you given him good reasons for liking the job and the organization?	___	___
(4) Have you prepared for his first day on the job?	___	___
(5) Did you welcome him cordially and make him feel needed?	___	___
(6) Did you establish rapport with him so that he feels free to talk and discuss matters with you?	___	___
(7) Did you explain his job to him and his relationship to you?	___	___
(8) Does he know that his work will be evaluated periodically on a basis that is fair and objective?	___	___
(9) Did you introduce him to his fellow workers in such a way that they are likely to accept him?	___	___
(10) Does he know what employee benefits he will receive?	___	___
(11) Does he understand the importance of being on the job and what to do if he must leave his duty station?	___	___
(12) Has he been impressed with the importance of accident prevention and safe practice?	___	___
(13) Does he generally know his way around the department?	___	___
(14) Is he under the guidance of a sponsor who will teach the right ways of doing things?	___	___
(15) Do you plan to follow-up so that he will continue to adjust successfully to his job?	___	___

19. *PRINCIPLES OF LEARNING*
      (1) Motivation   (2) Demonstration or explanation   (3) Practice

20. *CAUSES OF POOR PERFORMANCE*
      (1) Improper training for job
      (2) Wrong tools
      (3) Inadequate directions
      (4) Lack of supervisory follow-up
      (5) Poor communications
      (6) Lack of standards of performance
      (7) Wrong work habits
      (8) Low morale
      (9) Other

21. *FOUR MAJOR STEPS IN ON-THE-JOB INSTRUCTION*
      (1) Prepare the worker
      (2) Present the operation
      (3) Tryout performance
      (4) Follow-up

22. *EMPLOYEES WANT FIVE THINGS*
      (1) Security (2) Opportunity (3) Recognition (4) Inclusion (5) Expression

23. *SOME DON'TS IN REGARD TO PRAISE*
      (1) Don't praise a person for something he hasn't done
      (2) Don't praise a person unless you can be sincere
      (3) Don't be sparing in praise just because your superior withholds it from you
      (4) Don't let too much time elapse between good performance and recognition of it

24. *HOW TO GAIN YOUR WORKERS' CONFIDENCE*
Methods of developing confidence include such things as:
      (1) Knowing the interests, habits, hobbies of employees
      (2) Admitting your own inadequacies
      (3) Sharing and telling of confidence in others
      (4) Supporting people when they are in trouble
      (5) Delegating matters that can be well handled
      (6) Being frank and straightforward about problems and working conditions
      (7) Encouraging others to bring their problems to you
      (8) Taking action on problems which impede worker progress

25. *SOURCES OF EMPLOYEE PROBLEMS*
On-the-job causes might be such things as:
      (1) A feeling that favoritism is exercised in assignments
      (2) Assignment of overtime
      (3) An undue amount of supervision
      (4) Changing methods or systems
      (5) Stealing of ideas or trade secrets
      (6) Lack of interest in job
      (7) Threat of reduction in force
      (8) Ignorance or lack of communications
      (9) Poor equipment
      (10) Lack of knowing how supervisor feels toward employee
      (11) Shift assignments

Off-the-job problems might have to do with:
      (1) Health   (2) Finances   (3) Housing   (4) Family

26. THE SUPERVISOR'S KEY TO DISCIPLINE

There are several key points about discipline which the supervisor should keep in mind:
- (1) Job discipline is one of the disciplines of life and is directed by the supervisor.
- (2) It is more important to correct an employee fault than to fix blame for it.
- (3) Employee performance is affected by problems both on the job and off.
- (4) Sudden or abrupt changes in behavior can be indications of important employee problems.
- (5) Problems should be dealt with as soon as possible after they are identified.
- (6) The attitude of the supervisor may have more to do with solving problems than the techniques of problem solving.
- (7) Correction of employee behavior should be resorted to only after the supervisor is sure that training or counseling will not be helpful.
- (8) Be sure to document your disciplinary actions.
- (9) Make sure that you are disciplining on the basis of facts rather than personal feelings.
- (10) Take each disciplinary step in order, being careful not to make snap judgments, or decisions based on impatience.

27. FIVE IMPORTANT PROCESSES OF MANAGEMENT

- (1) Planning
- (2) Organizing
- (3) Scheduling
- (4) Controlling
- (5) Motivating

28. WHEN THE SUPERVISOR FAILS TO PLAN

- (1) Supervisor creates impression of not knowing his job
- (2) May lead to excessive overtime
- (3) Job runs itself -- supervisor lacks control
- (4) Deadlines and appointments missed
- (5) Parts of the work go undone
- (6) Work interrupted by emergencies
- (7) Sets a bad example
- (8) Uneven workload creates peaks and valleys
- (9) Too much time on minor details at expense of more important tasks

29. FOURTEEN GENERAL PRINCIPLES OF MANAGEMENT

- (1) Division of work
- (2) Authority and responsibility
- (3) Discipline
- (4) Unity of command
- (5) Unity of direction
- (6) Subordination of individual interest to general interest
- (7) Remuneration of personnel
- (8) Centralization
- (9) Scalar chain
- (10) Order
- (11) Equity
- (12) Stability of tenure of personnel
- (13) Initiative
- (14) Esprit de corps

30. CHANGE

Bringing about change is perhaps attempted more often, and yet less well understood, than anything else the supervisor does. How do people generally react to change? (People tend to resist change that is imposed upon them by other individuals or circumstances.

Change is characteristic of every situation. It is a part of every real endeavor where the efforts of people are concerned.

A. Why do people resist change?
   People may resist change because of:
   (1) Fear of the unknown
   (2) Implied criticism
   (3) Unpleasant experiences in the past
   (4) Fear of loss of status
   (5) Threat to the ego
   (6) Fear of loss of economic stability

B. How can we best overcome the resistance to change?
   In initiating change, take these steps:
   (1) Get ready to sell
   (2) Identify sources of help
   (3) Anticipate objections
   (4) Sell benefits
   (5) Listen in depth
   (6) Follow up

B. BRIEF TOPICAL SUMMARIES

I. WHO/WHAT IS THE SUPERVISOR?
1. The supervisor is often called the "highest level employee and the lowest level manager."
2. A supervisor is a member of both management and the work group. He acts as a bridge between the two.
3. Most problems in supervision are in the area of human relations, or people problems.
4. Employees expect: Respect, opportunity to learn and to advance, and a sense of belonging, and so forth.
5. Supervisors are responsible for directing people and organizing work. Planning is of paramount importance.
6. A position description is a set of duties and responsibilities inherent to a given position.
7. It is important to keep the position description up-to-date and to provide each employee with his own copy.

II. THE SOCIOLOGY OF WORK
1. People are alike in many ways; however, each individual is unique.
2. The supervisor is challenged in getting to know employee differences. Acquiring skills in evaluating individuals is an asset.
3. Maintaining meaningful working relationships in the organization is of great importance.
4. The supervisor has an obligation to help individuals to develop to their fullest potential.
5. Job rotation on a planned basis helps to build versatility and to maintain interest and enthusiasm in work groups.
6. Cross training (job rotation) provides backup skills.
7. The supervisor can help reduce tension by maintaining a sense of humor, providing guidance to employees, and by making reasonable and timely decisions. Employees respond favorably to working under reasonably predictable circumstances.
8. Change is characteristic of all managerial behavior. The supervisor must adjust to changes in procedures, new methods, technological changes, and to a number of new and sometimes challenging situations.
9. To overcome the natural tendency for people to resist change, the supervisor should become more skillful in initiating change.

III. PRINCIPLES AND PRACTICES OF SUPERVISION
1. Employees should be required to answer to only one superior.
2. A supervisor can effectively direct only a limited number of employees, depending upon the complexity, variety, and proximity of the jobs involved.
3. The organizational chart presents the organization in graphic form. It reflects lines of authority and responsibility as well as interrelationships of units within the organization.
4. Distribution of work can be improved through an analysis using the "Work Distribution Chart."
5. The "Work Distribution Chart" reflects the division of work within a unit in understandable form.
6. When related tasks are given to an employee, he has a better chance of increasing his skills through training.
7. The individual who is given the responsibility for tasks must also be given the appropriate authority to insure adequate results.
8. The supervisor should delegate repetitive, routine work. Preparation of recurring reports, maintaining leave and attendance records are some examples.
9. Good discipline is essential to good task performance. Discipline is reflected in the actions of employees on the job in the absence of supervision.
10. Disciplinary action may have to be taken when the positive aspects of discipline have failed. Reprimand, warning, and suspension are examples of disciplinary action.
11. If a situation calls for a reprimand, be sure it is deserved and remember it is to be done in private.

IV. DYNAMIC LEADERSHIP
1. A style is a personal method or manner of exerting influence.
2. Authoritarian leaders often see themselves as the source of power and authority.
3. The democratic leader often perceives the group as the source of authority and power.
4. Supervisors tend to do better when using the pattern of leadership that is most natural for them.
5. Social scientists suggest that the effective supervisor use the leadership style that best fits the problem or circumstances involved.
6. All four styles -- telling, selling, consulting, joining -- have their place. Using one does not preclude using the other at another time.
7. The theory X point of view assumes that the average person dislikes work, will avoid it whenever possible, and must be coerced to achieve organizational objectives.
8. The theory Y point of view assumes that the average person considers work to be as natural as play, and, when the individual is committed, he requires little supervision or direction to accomplish desired objectives.
9. The leader's basic assumptions concerning human behavior and human nature affect his actions, decisions, and other managerial practices.
10. Dissatisfaction among employees is often present, but difficult to isolate. The supervisor should seek to weaken dissatisfaction by keeping promises, being sincere and considerate, keeping employees informed, and so forth.
11. Constructive suggestions should be encouraged during the natural progress of the work.

V. PROCESSES FOR SOLVING PROBLEMS
1. People find their daily tasks more meaningful and satisfying when they can improve them.
2. The causes of problems, or the key factors, are often hidden in the background. Ability to solve problems often involves the ability to isolate them from their backgrounds. There is some substance to the cliché that some persons "can't see the forest for the trees."
3. New procedures are often developed from old ones. Problems should be broken down into manageable parts. New ideas can be adapted from old ones.

4. People think differently in problem-solving situations. Using a logical, patterned approach is often useful. One approach found to be useful includes these steps:
   - (a) Define the problem
   - (b) Establish objectives
   - (c) Get the facts
   - (d) Weigh and decide
   - (e) Take action
   - (f) Evaluate action

VI. TRAINING FOR RESULTS
1. Participants respond best when they feel training is important to them.
2. The supervisor has responsibility for the training and development of those who report to him.
3. When training is delegated to others, great care must be exercised to insure the trainer has knowledge, aptitude, and interest for his work as a trainer.
4. Training (learning) of some type goes on continually. The most successful supervisor makes certain the learning contributes in a productive manner to operational goals.
5. New employees are particularly susceptible to training. Older employees facing new job situations require specific training, as well as having need for development and growth opportunities.
6. Training needs require continuous monitoring.
7. The training officer of an agency is a professional with a responsibility to assist supervisors in solving training problems.
8. Many of the self-development steps important to the supervisor's own growth are equally important to the development of peers and subordinates. Knowledge of these is important when the supervisor consults with others on development and growth opportunities.

VII. HEALTH, SAFETY, AND ACCIDENT PREVENTION
1. Management-minded supervisors take appropriate measures to assist employees in maintaining health and in assuring safe practices in the work environment.
2. Effective safety training and practices help to avoid injury and accidents.
3. Safety should be a management goal. All infractions of safety which are observed should be corrected without exception.
4. Employees' safety attitude, training and instruction, provision of safe tools and equipment, supervision, and leadership are considered highly important factors which contribute to safety and which can be influenced directly by supervisors.
5. When accidents do occur they should be investigated promptly for very important reasons, including the fact that information which is gained can be used to prevent accidents in the future.

VIII. EQUAL EMPLOYMENT OPPORTUNITY
1. The supervisor should endeavor to treat all employees fairly, without regard to religion, race, sex, or national origin.
2. Groups tend to reflect the attitude of the leader. Prejudice can be detected even in very subtle form. Supervisors must strive to create a feeling of mutual respect and confidence in every employee.
3. Complete utilization of all human resources is a national goal. Equitable consideration should be accorded women in the work force, minority-group members, the physically and mentally handicapped, and the older employee. The important question is: "Who can do the job?"
4. Training opportunities, recognition for performance, overtime assignments, promotional opportunities, and all other personnel actions are to be handled on an equitable basis.

IX. IMPROVING COMMUNICATIONS

1. Communications is achieving understanding between the sender and the receiver of a message. It also means sharing information -- the creation of understanding.
2. Communication is basic to all human activity. Words are means of conveying meanings; however, real meanings are in people.
3. There are very practical differences in the effectiveness of one-way, impersonal, and two-way communications. Words spoken face-to-face are better understood. Telephone conversations are effective, but lack the rapport of person-to-person exchanges. The whole person communicates.
4. Cooperation and communication in an organization go hand in hand. When there is a mutual respect between people, spelling out rules and procedures for communicating is unnecessary.
5. There are several barriers to effective communications. These include failure to listen with respect and understanding, lack of skill in feedback, and misinterpreting the meanings of words used by the speaker. It is also common practice to listen to what we want to hear, and tune out things we do not want to hear.
6. Communication is management's chief problem. The supervisor should accept the challenge to communicate more effectively and to improve interagency and intra-agency communications.
7. The supervisor may often plan for and conduct meetings. The planning phase is critical and may determine the success or the failure of a meeting.
8. Speaking before groups usually requires extra effort. Stage fright may never disappear completely, but it can be controlled.

X. SELF-DEVELOPMENT

1. Every employee is responsible for his own self-development.
2. Toastmaster and toastmistress clubs offer opportunities to improve skills in oral communications.
3. Planning for one's own self-development is of vital importance. Supervisors know their own strengths and limitations better than anyone else.
4. Many opportunities are open to aid the supervisor in his developmental efforts, including job assignments; training opportunities, both governmental and non-governmental -- to include universities and professional conferences and seminars.
5. Programmed instruction offers a means of studying at one's own rate.
6. Where difficulties may arise from a supervisor's being away from his work for training, he may participate in televised home study or correspondence courses to meet his self-develop- ment needs.

XI. TEACHING AND TRAINING

A. The Teaching Process

Teaching is encouraging and guiding the learning activities of students toward established goals. In most cases this process consists in five steps: preparation, presentation, summarization, evaluation, and application.

1. Preparation

   Preparation is twofold in nature; that of the supervisor and the employee.
   Preparation by the supervisor is absolutely essential to success. He must know what, when, where, how, and whom he will teach. Some of the factors that should be considered are:

   (1) The objectives
   (2) The materials needed
   (3) The methods to be used
   (4) Employee participation
   (5) Employee interest
   (6) Training aids
   (7) Evaluation
   (8) Summarization

Employee preparation consists in preparing the employee to receive the material. Probably the most important single factor in the preparation of the employee is arousing and maintaining his interest. He must know the objectives of the training, why he is there, how the material can be used, and its importance to him.

2. Presentation

In presentation, have a carefully designed plan and follow it.
The plan should be accurate and complete, yet flexible enough to meet situations as they arise. The method of presentation will be determined by the particular situation and objectives.

3. Summary

A summary should be made at the end of every training unit and program. In addition, there may be internal summaries depending on the nature of the material being taught. The important thing is that the trainee must always be able to understand how each part of the new material relates to the whole.

4. Application

The supervisor must arrange work so the employee will be given a chance to apply new knowledge or skills while the material is still clear in his mind and interest is high. The trainee does not really know whether he has learned the material until he has been given a chance to apply it. If the material is not applied, it loses most of its value.

5. Evaluation

The purpose of all training is to promote learning. To determine whether the training has been a success or failure, the supervisor must evaluate this learning.

In the broadest sense evaluation includes all the devices, methods, skills, and techniques used by the supervisor to keep him self and the employees informed as to their progress toward the objectives they are pursuing. The extent to which the employee has mastered the knowledge, skills, and abilities, or changed his attitudes, as determined by the program objectives, is the extent to which instruction has succeeded or failed.

Evaluation should not be confined to the end of the lesson, day, or program but should be used continuously. We shall note later the way this relates to the rest of the teaching process.

B. Teaching Methods

A teaching method is a pattern of identifiable student and instructor activity used in presenting training material.
All supervisors are faced with the problem of deciding which method should be used at a given time.
As with all methods, there are certain advantages and disadvantages to each method.

1. Lecture

The lecture is direct oral presentation of material by the supervisor. The present trend is to place less emphasis on the trainer's activity and more on that of the trainee.

2. Discussion

Teaching by discussion or conference involves using questions and other techniques to arouse interest and focus attention upon certain areas, and by doing so creating a learning situation. This can be one of the most valuable methods because it gives the employees 'an opportunity to express their ideas and pool their knowledge.

3. Demonstration

The demonstration is used to teach how something works or how to do something. It can be used to show a principle or what the results of a series of actions will be. A well-staged demonstration is particularly effective because it shows proper methods of performance in a realistic manner.

4. Performance

Performance is one of the most fundamental of all learning techniques or teaching methods. The trainee may be able to tell how a specific operation should be performed but he cannot be sure he knows how to perform the operation until he has done so.

5. Which Method to Use

Moreover, there are other methods and techniques of teaching. It is difficult to use any method without other methods entering into it. In any learning situation a combination of methods is usually more effective than anyone method alone.

Finally, evaluation must be integrated into the other aspects of the teaching-learning process.

It must be used in the motivation of the trainees; it must be used to assist in developing understanding during the training; and it must be related to employee application of the results of training.

This is distinctly the role of the supervisor.

SUPERVISION STUDY GUIDE

Social science has developed information about groups and leadership in general and supervisor-employee relationships in particular. Since organizational effectiveness is closely linked to the ability of supervisors to direct the activities of employees, these findings are important to executives everywhere.

IS A SUPERVISOR A LEADER?

First-line supervisors are found in all large business and government organizations. They are the men at the base of an organizational hierarchy. Decisions made by the head of the organization reach them through a network of intermediate positions. They are frequently referred to as part of the management team, but their duties seldom seem to support this description.

A supervisor of clerks, tax collectors, meat inspectors, or securities analysts is not charged with budget preparation. He cannot hire or fire the employees in his own unit on his say-so. He does not administer programs which require great planning, coordinating, or decision making.

Then what is he? He is the man who is directly in charge of a group of employees doing productive work for a business or government agency. If the work requires the use of machines, the men he supervises operate them. If the work requires the writing of reports, the men he supervises write them. He is expected to maintain a productive flow of work without creating problems which higher levels of management must solve. But is he a leader?

To carry out a specific part of an agency's mission, management creates a unit, staffs it with a group of employees and designates a supervisor to take charge of them. Management directs what this unit shall do, from time to time changes directions, and often indicates what the group should not do. Management presumably creates status for the supervisor by giving him more pay, a title, and special priviledges.

Management asks a supervisor to get his workers to attain organizational goals, including the desired quantity and quality of production. Supposedly, he has authority to enable him to achieve this objective. Management at least assumes that by establishing the status of the supervisor's position it has created sufficient authority to enable him to achieve these goals -- not his goals, nor necessarily the group's, but management's goals.

In addition, supervision includes writing reports, keeping records of membership in a higher-level administrative group, industrial engineering, safety engineering, editorial duties, housekeeping duties, etc. The supervisor as a member of an organizational network, must be responsible to the changing demands of the management above him. At the same time, he must be responsive to the demands of the work group of which he is a member. He is placed in the difficult position of communicating and implementing new decisions, changed programs and revised production quotas for his work group, although he may have had little part in developing them.

It follows, then, that supervision has a special characteristic: achievement of goals, previously set by management, through the efforts of others. It is in this feature of the supervisor's job that we find the role of a leader in the sense of the following definition: *A leader is that person who <u>most</u> effectively influences group activities toward goal setting and goal achievements.*

This definition is broad. It covers both leaders in groups that come together voluntarily and in those brought together through a work assignment in a factory, store, or government agency. In the natural group, the authority necessary to attain goals is determined by the group membership and is granted by them. In the working group, it is apparent that the establishment of a supervisory position creates a predisposition on the part of employees to accept the authority of the occupant of that position. We cannot, however, assume that mere occupancy confers authority sufficient to assure the accomplishment of an organization's goals.

Supervision is different, then, from leadership. The supervisor is expected to fulfill the role of leader but without obtaining a grant of authority from the group he supervises. The supervisor is expected to influence the group in the achieving of goals but is often handicapped by having little influence on the organizational process by which goals are set. The supervisor, because he works in an organizational setting, has the burdens of additional organizational duties and restrictions and requirements arising out of the fact that his position is subordinate to a hierarchy of higher-level supervisors. These differences between leadership and supervision are reflected in our definition: *Supervision is basically a leadership role, in a formal organization, which has as its objective the effective influencing of other employees.*

Even though these differences between supervision and leadership exist, a significant finding of experimenters in this field is that supervisors <u>must</u> be leaders to be successful.

The problem is: How can a supervisor exercise leadership in an organizational setting? We might say that the supervisor is expected to be a natural leader in a situation which does not come about naturally. His situation becomes really difficult in an organization which is more eager to make its supervisors into followers rather than leaders.

LEADERSHIP: NATURAL AND ORGANIZATIONAL

Leadership, in its usual sense of *natural* leadership, and supervision are not the same. In some cases, leadership embraces broader powers and functions than supervision; in other cases, supervision embraces more than leadership. This is true both because of the organization and technical aspects of the supervisor's job and because of the relatively freer setting and inherent authority of the natural leader.

The natural leader usually has much more authority and influence than the supervisor. Group members not only follow his command but prefer it that way. The employee, however, can appeal the supervisor's commands to his union or to the supervisor's superior or to the personnel office. These intercessors represent restrictions on the supervisor's power to lead.

The natural leader can gain greater membership involvement in the group's objectives, and he can change the objectives of the group. The supervisor can attempt to gain employee support only for management's objectives; he cannot set other objectives. In these instances leadership is broader than supervision.

The natural leader must depend upon whatever skills are available when seeking to attain objectives. The supervisor is trained in the administrative skills necessary to achieve management's goals. If he does not possess the requisite skills, however, he can call upon management's technicians.

A natural leader can maintain his leadership, in certain groups, merely by satisfying members' need for group affilation. The supervisor must maintain his leadership by directing and organizing his group to achieve specific organizational goals set for him and his group by management. He must have a technical competence and a kind of coordinating ability which is not needed by many natural leaders.

A natural leader is responsible only to his group which grants him authority. The supervisor is responsible to management, which employs him, and, also, to the work group of which he is a member. The supervisor has the exceedingly difficult job of reconciling the demands of two groups frequently in conflict. He is often placed in the untenable position of trying to play two antagonisic roles. In the above instances, supervision is broader than leadership.

ORGANIZATIONAL INFLUENCES ON LEADERSHIP

The supervisor is both a product and a prisoner of the organization wherein we find him. The organization which creates the supervisor's position also obstructs, restricts, and channelizes the exercise of his duties. These influences extend beyond prescribed functional relationships to specific supervisory behavior. For example, even in a face-to-face situation involving one of his subordinates, the supervisor's actions are controlled to a great extent by his organization. His behavior must conform to the organization policy on human relations, rules which dictate personnel procedures, specific prohibitions governing conduct, the attitudes of his own superior, etc. He is not a free agent operating within the limits of his work group. His freedom of action is much more circumscribed than is generally admitted. The organizational influences which limit his leadership actions can be classified as structure, prescriptions, and proscriptions.

The organizational structure places each supervisor's position in context with other designated positions. It determines the relationships between his position and specific positions which impinge on his. The structure of the organization designates a certain position to which he looks for orders and information about his work. It gives a particular status to his position within a pattern of statuses from which he perceives that (1) certain positions are on a par, organizationally, with his, (2) other positions are subordinate, and (3) still others are superior. The organizational structure determines those positions to which he should look for advice and assistance, and those positions to which he should give advice and assistance.

For instance, the organizational structure has predetermined that the supervisor of a clerical processing unit shall report to a supervisory position in a higher echelon. He shall have certain relationships with the supervisors of the work units which transmit work to and receive work from his unit. He shall discuss changes and clarification of procedures with certain staff units, such as organization and methods, cost accounting, and personnel. He shall consult supervisors of units which provide or receive special work assignments.

The organizational structure, however, establishes patterns other than those of the relationships of positions. These are the patterns of responsibility, authority, and expectations.

The supervisor is responsible for certain activities or results; he is presumably invested with the authority to achieve these. His set of authority and responsibility is interwoven with other sets to the end that all goals and functions of the organization are parceled out in small, manageable lots. This, of course, establishes a series of expectations: a single supervisor can perform his particular set of duties only upon the assumption that preceding or contiguous sets of duties have been, or are being, carried out. At the same time, he is aware of the expectations of others that he will fulfill his functional role.

The structure of an organization establishes relationships between specified positions and specific expectations for these positions. The fact that these relationships and expectations are established is one thing; whether or not they are met is another.

PRESCRIPTIONS AND PROSCRIPTIONS

But let us return to the organizational influences which act to restrict the supervisor's exercise of leadership. These are the prescriptions and proscriptions generally in effect in all organizations, and those peculiar to a single organization. In brief these are the *thous shalt's* and the *thou shalt not's*.

Organizations not only prescribe certain duties for individual supervisory positions, they also prescribe specific methods and means of carrying out these duties and maintaining management-employee relations. These include rules, regulations, policy, and. tradition. It does no good for the supervisor to say, *This seems to be the best way to handle such-and such,* if the organization has established a routine for dealing with problems. For good or bad, there are rules that state that firings shall be executed in such a manner, accompanied by a certain notification; that training shall be conducted, and in this manner. Proscriptions are merely negative prescriptions: you may not discriminate against any employee because of politics or race; you shall not suspend any employee without following certain procedures and obtaining certain approvals.

Most of these prohibitions and rules apply to the area of interpersonal relations, precisely the area which is now arousing most interest on the part of administrators and managers. We have become concerned about the contrast between formally prescribed relationships and interpersonal relationships, and this brings us to the often discussed informal organization.

FORMAL AND INFORMAL ORGANIZATIONS

As we well know, the functions and activities of any organization are broken down into individual units of work called positions. Administrators must establish a pattern which will link these positions to each other and relate them to a system of authority and responsibility. Man-to-man are spelled out as plainly as possible for all to understand. Managers, then, build an official structure which we call the formal organization.

In these same organizations employees react individually and in groups to institutionally determined roles. John, a worker, rides in the same car pool as Joe, a foreman. An unplanned communication develops. Harry, a machinist, knows more about highspeed machining than his foreman or anyone else in his shop. An unofficial tool boss comes into being. Mary, who fought with Jane is promoted over her. Jane now ignores Mary's directions. A planned relationship fails to develop. The employees have built a structure which we call the informal organization.

Formal organization is a system of management-prescribed relations between positions in an organization.

Informal organization is a network of unofficial relations between people in an organization.

These definitions might lead us to the absurd conclusion that positions carry out formal activities and that employees spend their time in unofficial activities. We must recognize that organizational activities are in all cases carried out by people. The formal structure provides a needed framework within which interpersonal relations occur. What we call informal organization is the complex of normal, natural relations among employees. These personal relationships may be negative or positive. That is, they may impede or aid the achievement of organizational, goals. For example, friendship between two supervisors greatly increases the probability of good cooperation and coordination between their sections. On the other hand, *buck passing* nullifies the formal structure by failure to meet a prescribed and expected responsibility.

It is improbable that an ideal organization exists where all activities are acarried out in strict conformity to a formally prescribed pattern of functional roles. Informal organization arises because of the incompleteness and ambiguities in the network of formally prescribed relationships, or in response to the needs or inadequacies of supervisors or managers who hold prescribed functional roles in an organization. Many of these relationships are not prescribed by the organizational pattern; many cannot be prescribed; many should not be prescribed.

Management faces the problem of keeping the informal organization in harmony with the mission of the agency. One way to do this is to make sure that all employees have a clear understanding of and are sympathetic with that mission. The issuance of organizational charts, procedural manuals, and functional descriptions of the work to be done by divisions and sections helps communicate management's plans and goals. Issuances alone, of course, cannot do the whole job. They should be accompanied by oral discussion and explanation. Management must ensure that there is mutual understanding and acceptance of charts and procedures. More important is that management acquaint itself with the attitudes, activities, and peculiar brands of logic which govern the informal organization. Only through this type of knowledge can they and supervisors keep informal goals consistent with the agency mission.

SUPERVISION, STATUS, AND FUNCTIONAL ROLE

A well-established supervisor is respected by the employees who work with him. They defer to his wishes. It is clear that a superior-subordinate relationship has been established. That is, status of the supervisor has been established in relation to other employees of the same work group. This same supervisor gains the respect of employees when he behaves in a certain manner. He will be expected generally, to follow the customs of the group in such matters as dress, recreation, and manner of speaking. The group has a set of expectations as to his behavior. His position is a functional role which carries with it a collection of rights and obligations.

The position of supervisor usually has a status distinct from the individual who occupies it: it is much like a position description which exists whether or not there is an incumbent. The status of a supervisory position is valued higher than that of an employee position both because of the functional role of leadership which is assigned to it and because of the status symbols of titles, rights, and privileges which go with it.

Social ranking, or status, is not simple because it involves both the position and the man. An individual may be ranked higher than others because of his education, social background, perceived leadership ability, or conformity to group customs and ideals. If such a man is ranked higher by the members of a work group than their supervisor, the supervisor's effectiveness may be seriously undermined.

If the organization does not build and reinforce a supervisor's status, his position can be undermined in a different way. This will happen when managers go around rather than through the supervisor or designate him as a straw boss, acting boss, or otherwise not a real boss.

Let us clarify this last point. A role, and corresponding status, establishes a set of expectations. Employees expect their supervisor to do certain things and to act in certain ways. They are prepared to respond to that expected behavior. When the supervisor's behavior does not conform to their expectations, they are surprised, confused, and ill-at-ease. It becomes necessary for them to resolve their confusion, if they can. They might do this by turning to one of their own members for leadership. If the confusion continues, or their attempted solutions are not satisfactory, they will probably become a poorly motivated, non-cohesive group which cannot function very well.

COMMUNICATION AND THE SUPERVISOR

In a recent survey railroad workers reported that they rarely look to their supervisors for information about the company. This is startling, at least to us, because we ordinarily think of the supervisor as the link between management and worker. We expect the supervisor to be the prime source of information about the company. Actually, the railroad workers listed the supervisor next to last in the order of their sources of information. Most suprising of all, the supervisors, themselves, stated that rumor and unofficial contacts were their principal sources of information. Here we see one of the reasons why supervisors may not be as effective as management desires.

The supervisor is not only being bypassed by his work group, he is being ignored, and his position weakened, by the very organization which is holding him responsible for the activities of his workers. If he is management's representative to the employee, then management has an obligation to keep him informed of its activities. This is necessary if he is to carry out his functions efficiently and maintain his leadership in the work group. The supervisor is expected to be a source of information; when he is not, his status is not clear, and employees are dissatisfied because he has not lived up to expectations.

By providing information to the supervisor to pass along to employees, we can strengthen his position as leader of the group, and increase satisfaction and cohesion within the group. Because he has more information than the other members, receives information sooner, and passes it along at the proper times, members turn to him as a source and also provide him with information in the hope of receiving some in return. From this we can see an increase in group cohesiveness because:

- o   Employees are bound closer to their supervisor because he is *in the know*

- o   there is less need to go outside the group for answers

- o   employees will more quickly turn to the supervisor for enlightenment.

The fact that he has the answers will also enhance the supervisor's standing in the eyes of his men. This increased sta,tus will serve to bolster his authority and control of the group and will probably result in improved morale and productivity.

The foregoing, of course, does not mean that all management information should be given out. There are obviously certain policy determinations and discussions which need not or cannot be transmitted to all supervisors. However, the supervisor must be kept as fully informed as possible so that he can answer questions when asked and can allay needless fears and anxieties. Further, the supervisor has the responsibility of encouraging employee questions and submissions of information. He must be able to present information to employees so that it is clearly understood and accepted. His attitude and manner should make it clear that he believes in what he is saying, that the information is necessary or desirable to the group, and that he is prepared to act on the basis of the information.

SUPERVISION AND JOB PERFORMANCE

The productivity of work groups is a product; employees' efforts are multiplied by the supervision they receive. Many investigators have analyzed this relationship and have discovered elements of supervision which differentiate high and low production groups. These researchers have identified certain types of supervisory practices which they classify as *employee-centered* and other types which they classify as *production centered*.

The difference between these two kinds of supervision lies not in specific practices but in the approach or orientation to supervision. The employee-centered supervisor directs most of his efforts toward increasing employee motivation. He is concerned more with realizing the potential energy of persons than with administrative and technological methods of increasing efficiency and productivity. He is the man who finds ways of causing employees to want to work harder with the same tools. These supervisors emphasize the personal relations between their employees and themselves.

Now, obviously, these pictures are overdrawn. No one supervisor has all the virtues of the ideal type of employee-centered supervisor. And, fortunately, no one supervisor has all the bad traits found in many production-centered supervisors. We should remember that the various practices that researchers have found which distinguish these two kinds of supervision represent the many practices and methods of supervisors of all gradations between these extremes. We should be careful, too, of the implications of the labels attached to the two types. For instance, being production-centered is not necessarily bad, since the principal responsibility of any supervisor is maintaining the production level that is expected of his work group. Being employee-centered may not necessarily be good, if the only result is a happy, chuckling crew of loafers. To return to the researchers's findings, employee-centered supervisors:

- Recommend promotions, transfers, pay increases
- Inform men about what is happening in the company
- Keep men posted on how well they are doing
- Hear complaints and grievances sympathetically
- Speak up for subordinates

Production-centered supervisors, on the other hand, don't do those things. They check on employees more frequently, give more detailed and frequent instructions, don't give reasons for changes, and are more punitive when mistakes are made. Employee-centered supervisors were reported to contribute to high morale and high production, whereas production-centered supervision was associated with lower morale and less production.

More recent findings, however, show that the relationship between supervision and productivity is not this simple. Investigators now report that high production is more frequently associated with supervisory practices which combine employee-centered behavior with concern for production. (This concern is not the same, however, as anxiety about production, which is the hallmark of our production-centered supervisor.) Let us examine these apparently contradictory findings and the premises from which they are derived.

SUPERVISION AND MORALE

Why do supervisory activities cause high or low production? As the name implies, the activities of the employee-centered supervisor tend to relate him more closely and satisfactorily to his workers. The production-centered supervisor's practices tend to separate him from his group and to foster antagonism. An analysis of this difference may answer our question.

Earlier, we pointed out that the supervisor is a type of leader and that leadership is intimately related to the group in which it occurs. We discover, now, that an employee-centered supervisor's primary activities are concerned with both his leadership and his group membership. Such a supervisor is a member of a group and occupies a leadership role in that group.

These facts are sometimes obscured when we speak of the supervisor as management's representative, or as the organizational link between management and the employee, or as the end of the chain of command. If we really want to understand what it is we expect of the supervisor, we must remember that he is the designated leader of a group of employees to whom he is bound by interaction and interdependence.

Most of his actions are aimed, consciously or unconsciously, at strengthening membership ties in the group. This includes both making members more conscious that he is a member of their grout) and causing members to identify themselves more closely with the group. These ends are accomplished by:

>   making the group more attractive to the worker: they
>   find satisfaction of their needs for recognition,
>   friendship, enjoyable work, etc.;
>
>   maintaining open communication: employees can express
>   their views and obtain information about the organization.
>
>   giving assistance: members can seek advice on
>   personal problems as well as their work; and
>   acting as a buffer between the group and management:
>   he speaks up for his men and explains the reasons
>   for management's decisions.

Such actions both strengthen group cohesiveness and solidarity and affirm the supervisor's leadership position in the group.

DEFINING MORALE

This brings us back to a point mentioned earlier. We had said that employee-centered supervisors contribute to high morale as well as to high production. But how can we explain units which have low morale and high productivity, or vice versa? Usually production and morale are considered separately, partly because they are measured against different criteria and partly because, in some instances, they seem to be independent of each other.

Some of this difficulty may stem from confusion over definitions of morale. Morale has been defined as, or measured by, absences from work, satisfaction with job or company, dissension among members of work groups, productivity, apathy or lack of interest, readiness to help others, and a general aura of happiness as rated by observers. Some of these criteria of morale are not subject to the influence of the supervisor, and some of them are not clearly related to productivity. Definitions like these invite findings of low morale coupled with high production.

Both productivity and morale can be influenced by environmental factors not under the control of group members or supervisors. Such things as plant layout, organizational structure and goals, lighting, ventilation, communications, and management planning may have an adverse or desirable effect.

We might resolve the dilemma by defining morale on the basis of our understanding of the supervisor as leader of a group; morale is the degree of satisfaction of group members with their leadership. In this light, the supervisor's employee-centered activities bear a clear relation to morale. His efforts to increase employee identification with the group and to strengthen his leadership lead to greater satisfaction with that leadership. By increasing group cohesiveness and by demonstrating that his influence and power can aid the group, he is able to enhance his leadership status and afford satisfaction to the group.

SUPERVISION, PRODUCTION, AND MORALE

There are factors within the organization itself which determine whether increased production is possible:

Are production goals expressed in terms understandable to employees and are they realistic?

Do supervisors responsible for production respect the agency mission and production goals?

If employees do not know how to do the job well, does management provide a trainer--often the supervisor--who can teach efficient work methods?

There are other factors within the work group which determine whether increased production will be attained:

Is leadership present which can bring about the desired level of production?

Are production goals accepted by employees as reasonable and attainable?

If group effort is involved, are members able to coordinate their efforts?

Research findings confirm the view that an employee-centered supervisor can achieve higher morale than a production-centered supervisor. Managers may well ask what is the relationship between this and production?

Supervision is production-oriented to the extent that it focuses attention on achieving organizational goals, and plans and devises methods for attaining them; it is employee-centered to the extent that it focuses attention on employee attitudes toward those goals, and plans and works toward maintenance of employee satisfaction.

High productivity and low morale result when a supervisor plans and organizes work efficiently but cannot achieve high membership satisfaction. Low production and high morale result when a supervisor, though keeping members satisfied with his leadership, either has not gained acceptance of organizational goals or does not have the technical competence to achieve them.

The relationship between supervision, morale, and productivity is an interdependent one, with the supervisor playing an integrating role due to his ability to influence productivity and morale independently of each other.

A supervisor who can plan his work well has good technical knowledge, and who can install better production methods can raise production without necessarily increasing group satisfaction. On the other hand, a supervisor who can motivate his employees and keep them satisfied with his leadership can gain high production in spite of technical difficulties and environmental obstacles.

CLIMATE AND SUPERVISION

Climate, the intangible environment of an organization made up of attitudes, beliefs, and traditions, plays a large part in morale, productivity, and supervision. Usually when we speak of climate and its relationship to morale and productivity, we talk about the merits of *democratic* versus *authoritarian* climate. Employees seem to produce more and have higher morale in a democratic climate, whereas in an authoritarian climate, the reverse seems to be true or so the researchers tell us. We would do well to determine what these terms mean to supervision.

Perhaps most of our difficulty in understanding and applying these concepts comes from our emotional reactions to the words themselves. For example, authoritarian climate is usually painted as the very blackest kind of dictatorship. This not surprising, because we are usually expected to believe that it is invariably bad. Conversely, democratic climate is drawn to make the driven snow look impure by comparison.

Now these descriptions are most probably true when we talk about our political processes, or town meetings, or freedom of speech. However the same labels have been used by social scientists in other contexts and have also been applied to government and business organizations, without, it seems, any recognition that the meanings and their social values may have changed somewhat .

For example, these labels were used in experiments conducted in an informal class room setting using 11 year old boys as subjects. The descriptive labels applied to the climate of the setting as well as the type of leadership practiced. When these labels were transferred to a management setting it seems that many presumed that they principally meant the king of leadership rather than climate. We can see that there is a great difference between the experimental and management settings and that leadership practices for one might be inappropriate for the other.

It is doubtful that formal work organizations can be anything but authoritarian, in that goals are set by management and a hierarchy exists through which decisions and orders from the top are transmitted downward. Organizations are authoritarian by structure and need: direction and control are placed in the hands of a few in order to gain fast and efficient decision making. Now this does not mean to describe a dictatorship. It is merely the recognition of the fact that direction of organizational affairs comes from above. It should be noted that leadership in some natural groups is, in this sense, authoritarian.

Granting that formal organizations have this kind of authoritarian leadership, can there be a democratic climate? Certainly there can be, but we would want to define and delimit this term. A more realistic meaning of democratic climate in organizations is, the use of permissive and participatory methods in management-employee relations. That is, a mutual exchange of information and explanation with the granting of individual freedom within certain restricted and defined limits. However, it is not our purpose to debate the merits of authoritarianism versus democracy. We recognize that within the small work group there is a need for freedom from constraint and an increase in participation in order to achieve organizational goals within the framework of the organizational environment.

Another aspect of climate is best expressed by this familiar, and true saying: actions speak louder than words. Of particular concern to us is this effect of management climate on the behavior of supervisors, particularly in employee-centered activities.

There have been reports of disappointment with efforts to make supervisors more employee-centered. Managers state that, since research has shown ways of improving human relations, supervisors should begin to practice these methods. Usually a training course in human relations is established, and supervisors are given this training. Managers then sit back and wait for the expected improvements, only to find that there are none.

If we wish to produce changes in the supervisor's behavior, the climate must be made appropriate and rewarding to the changed behavior. This means that top-level attitudes and behavior cannot deny or contradict the change we are attempting to effect. Basic changes in organizational behavior cannot be made with any permanence, unless we provide an environment that is receptive to the changes and rewards those persons who do change.

IMPROVING SUPERVISION

Anyone who has read this far might expect to find *A Dozen Rules for Dealing With Employees* or *29 Steps to Supervisory Success.* We will not provide such a list.

Simple rules suffer from their simplicity. They ignore the complexities of human behavior. Reliance upon rules may cause supervisors to concentrate on superficial aspects of their relations with employees. It may preclude genuine understanding.

The supervisor who relies on a list of rules tends to think of people in mechanistic terms. In a certain situation, he uses *Rule No. 3*. Employees are not treated as thinking and feeling persons, but rather as figures in a formula: Rule 3 applied to employee X = Production.

Employees usually recognize mechanical manipulation and become dissatisfied and resentful. They lose faith in, and respect for, their supervisor, and this may be reflected in lower morale and productivity.

We do not mean that supervisors must become social science experts if they wish to improve. Reports of current research indicate that there are two major parts of their job which can be strengthened through self-improvement: (1) Work planning, including technical skills. (2) Motivation of employees.

The most effective supervisors combine excellence in the administrative and technical aspects of their work with friendly and considerate personal relations with their employees.

CRITICAL PERSONAL RELATIONS

Later in this chaper we shall talk about administrative aspects of supervision, but first let us comment on *friendly and considerate personal relations*. We have discussed this subject throughout the preceding chapters, but we want to review some of the critical supervisory influences on personal relations.

Closeness of Supervision

The closeness of supervision has an important effect on productivity and morale. Mann and Dent found that supervisors of low-producing units supervise very closely, while high-producing supervisors exercise only general supervision. It was found that the low-producing supervisors:

- o   check on employees more frequently
- o   give more detailed and frequent instructions
- o   limit employee's freedom to do job in own way.

Workers who felt less closely supervised reported that they were better satisfied with their jobs and the company. We should note that the manner or attitude of the supervisor has an important bearing on whether employees perceive supervision as being close or general.

These findings are another way of saying that supervision does not mean standing over the employee and telling him what to do and when and how to do it. The more effective supervisor tells his employees what is required, giving general instructions.

COMMUNICATION

Supervisors of high-production units consider communication as one of the most important aspects of their job. Effective communication is used by these supervisors to achieve better interpersonal relations and improved employee motivation. Low-production supervisors do not rate communication as highly important.

High-producing supervisors find that an important aid to more effective communication is listening. They are ready to listen to both personal problems or interests and questions about the work. This does not mean that they are *nosey* or meddle in their employees' personal lives, but rather that they show a willingness to listen, and do listen, if their employees wish to discuss problems.

These supervisors inform employees about forthcoming changes in work; they discuss agency policy with employees; and they make sure that each employee knows how well he is doing. What these supervisors do is use two-way communication effectively. Unless the supervisor freely imparts information, he will not receive information in return.

Attitudes and perception are frequently affected by communication or the lack of it. Research surveys reveal that many supervisors are not aware of their employees' attitudes, nor do they know what personal reactions their supervision arouses. Through frank discussions with employees, they have been surprised to discover employee beliefs about which they were ignorant. Discussion sometimes reveals that the supervisor and his employees have totally different impressions about the same event. The supervisor should be constantly on the alert for misconceptions about his words and deeds. He must remember that, although his actions are perfectly clear to himself, they may be, and frequently are, viewed differently by employees.

Failure to communicate information results in misconceptions and false assumptions. What you say and how you say it will strongly affect your employees' attitudes and perceptions. By giving them available information you can prevent misconceptions; by discussion, you may be able to change attitudes; by questioning; you can discover what the perceptions and assumptions really are. And it need hardly be added that actions should conform very closely to words.

If we were to attempt to reduce the above discussion on communication to rules, we would have a long list which would be based on one cardinal principle: Don't make assumptions!
- Don't assume that your employees know; tell them.
- Don't assume that you know how they feel; find out.
- Don't assume that they understand; clarify.

20 SUPERVISORY HINTS

1. Avoid inconsistency.
2. Always give employees a chance to explain their actions before taking disciplinary action. Don't allow too much time for a "cooling off" period before disciplining an employee.
3. Be specific in your criticisms.
4. Delegate responsibility wisely.
5. Do not argue or lose your temper, and avoid being impatient.
6. Promote mutual respect and be fair, impartial and open-minded.
7. Keep in mind that asking for employees' advice and input can be helpful in decision making.
8. If you make promises, keep them.
9. Always keep the feelings, abilities, dignity and motives of your staff in mind.
10. Remain loyal to your employees' interests.
11. Never criticize employees in front of others, or treat employees like children.
12. Admit mistakes. Don't place blame on your employees, or make excuses.
13. Be reasonable in your expectations, give complete instructions, and establish well-planned goals.
14. Be knowledgeable about office details and procedures, but avoid becoming bogged down in details.
15. Avoid supervising too closely or too loosely. Employees should also view you as an approachable supervisor.
16. Remember that employees' personal problems may affect job performance, but become involved only when appropriate.
17. Work to develop workers, and to instill a feeling of cooperation while working toward mutual goals.
18. Do not overpraise or underpraise, be properly appreciative.
19. Never ask an employee to discipline someone for you.
20. A complaint, even if unjustified, should be taken seriously.